Foreword

Empowerment has been one of the most far-reaching social trends during my lifetime - being better informed, guided or advised to make decisions.

More than ever before, I see individuals and families taking responsibility for their lives. People expect to be actively involved in the vital decisions that affect their future. Information that was once reserved for highly trained professionals is now readily available, partly through the general proliferation of media, and in particular through the rise of the digital age. So whether the choice being faced relates to the care of aging relatives, or the education of children, or financial well-being, the theme of *empowerment* is ever-present in our lives. These issues are too important for the decision to be delegated to remote bureaucrats. People yearn to understand the issues, and to work closely with subject matter professions on the solution that's right for them.

I have touched on financial well-being, and of course we are fortunate to live in an era of relative wealth. Yet, with rising prosperity brings new challenges. We are living longer, and a larger proportion of our lives will be spent in retirement. Government austerity programmes are encouraging greater self-reliance. Reforms to the annuity market have created an abundance of options about matters that were once more straightforward. The modern consumer of financial services is, truly, an empowered consumer.

These trends have a dramatic impact on the role of the professional financial planner. It is now mission critical to work in partnership with each client to find the solution that's best for them and their families. Skills such as listening, creativity and judgement are more significant than ever. They mean the planner can operate as an enabler of empowerment, not a barrier to it. Robin Melley's thought-provoking book - packed with facts, case studies and anecdotes - is a timely reminder of these essential principles. I commend the author for so properly and courageously placing empowerment at the very heart of his six stage programme.

Keith Richards – CEO of The Personal Finance Society

Acknowledgements

This is my first book and, although I'm passionate about the subject, I accept that I'm too close to the issues and accept that that might cause me to "not see the wood for the trees". So, I am extremely grateful for the brutally honest feedback on the original iteration from a number of people:

Tim Middleham – CEO, CML.

Tim is an entrepreneur and CEO of a highly successful logistics business. To use his words he likes to, "...call a spade a shovel!"

His overall summary of the first draft of the book was that I'd lost my way half way through. So, thank you for pointing that out; and hopefully, I have addressed that point and written something that does have a logical and engaging progression from one chapter to the next.

Thanks Tim!

Tim Thackrah – Owner, Elmsleigh House Dental Clinic

Although Tim is a highly qualified and eminent dentist, he is a rare breed amongst dentists in that he has demonstrated that he has entrepreneurial flair and the ability to build a portfolio of highly successful businesses in other areas such as training and architecture.

I am indebted to Tim for his valuable insights and suggestions from the perspective of a potential reader but also as a successful businessman and author. His frank and forthright feedback has been invaluable and I thank him for that.

Andrew Mason – Independent Chair of The Safeguarding Children Board.

Andrew is what I refer to as a modern day "Sage", who is blessed with an innate wisdom to immediately identify the common-sense approach to situations.

His opening comment about the first draft was, "...is it a self-help volume or a promotional tool for your business model?"

A good question, which I hope I've addressed. I definitely wanted the book to be a useful resource for the reader and not a promotion for my business. That said, a lot of the wisdom that I've attempted to pass on in the book has been developed as a result of meeting lots of clients through my business.

Hopefully, I've got the messages across without turning it into an advertisement for my Company – you'll be the judge of that.

Paul Thomas – Managing Director & Wealth Coach, Generic Financial Management Plc.

I first met Paul at The Strategic Coach® workshops in London in 2006 and we immediately hit it off. I have immense respect and admiration for Paul – he is hugely successful both as a professional financial planner and as an entrepreneur and a thoroughly decent person.

Paul has innovated many things in the profession of financial planning and has intimate knowledge of the types of people who are likely to read this book, which has undoubtedly helped to make the content relevant and informative.

Gary Matthews – Chartered Financial Planner and Director, Matrix Capital Limited.

Gary has been my business partner since 2008. He is one of the highest qualified financial planners in the UK and is a Fellow of The Personal Finance Society. He has a very logical and precise way of working and has a "no nonsense" approach with people, which is very refreshing. He will always tell the way it is rather than the way you'd like it to be.

His insights and support in writing this book have been brilliant; and I really appreciate his intellect and his honest feedback.

May I also take this opportunity to share with you that we are proud supporters of Ladies Fighting Breast Cancer (LFBC), a voluntary group of ladies who donate their time and services to raise funds and awareness of Breast Cancer in the West Midlands. Established in 2000 by Veronica Kumeta and the late Sue Macmaster, their success and achievements have been fantastic, however there is still much to do. We are pleased to be donating all revenue we receive from this book to this worthy cause and we encourage your further support.

You can find out more about LFBC by visiting their website: www.ladiesfightingbreastcancer.org.uk.

Contents

	Page
Introduction	6
The Exploratory Meeting	10
Chapter 1: Stage 1 - The Clarity Builder™	19
Chapter 2: Stage 2 - The Gap Analysis™	26
Chapter 3: Stage 3 - The Strategy Platform™	41
Chapter 4: Stage 4 - The Implementation Planner™	60
Chapter 5: Stage 5 - The Impact Report™	71
Chapter 6: Stage 6 - The Planning Review Programme™	73
Chapter 7: Family Financial Planning	81
Chapter 8: Some Financial Explanations	85
Chapter 9: Tax Planning	92
Summary	97
Glossary	98
Real Life Case Studies	111
Notes Space	120

Introduction

Why should you read this book?

The simple answer to that question is that; you don't know what you don't know; and if you did know, you would be in a far better overall financial position.

Having been involved in financial services and the financial planning profession since 1991, I have reached the conclusion that most people have ended up being disenfranchised when it comes to personal financial planning. This is admittedly in part due to the various miss-selling scandals that have occurred over the last 30 years, which may have caused many people to shy away from taking professional advice.

The question I would ask those people is, "did you stop going to your GP because you read about the rogue doctor, Harold Shipman?"

There have been significant changes in the world of financial planning and financial advice over the last 25 years. The most recent development has been the implementation of the Retail Distribution Review (RDR) that occurred at midnight on 31st December 2012.

Amongst other things, RDR replaced commission paid on the sale of investment and pension products with 'Adviser Charging', which means that all advisers are now required to do what professional financial planners have been doing for years – agree a transparent fee arrangement with you for advice, implementation and on-going service. The other big change is that investment advisers are now required to have a QCF Level 4 qualification instead of the previous Level 3 requirement.

RDR is discussed in greater detail later on, but the big picture with RDR is that its aim was to create greater transparency and raise standards of professionalism in financial advice and financial planning.

The truth is that there is a danger that thousands of people continue to live with false beliefs about working with a financial adviser and a financial planner and, in consequence, mask the fact that the investment performance on their savings, investments and pensions is terrible, their portfolio is a mess and in the wrong structure and they are setting themselves up to pay significantly more tax than they would otherwise pay with proper planning.

My hope is that this book will act as a catalyst for positive change for you the reader; and it will lead you to understand the logical steps that professional and ethical financial planners take in order to achieve long-term results for their clients, without taking uncomfortable risks. Your hard earned wealth will hopefully be better structured, your financial affairs simplified and organised, investment results improved upon and you will know how to pay only the amount of tax that the law requires you to pay; and I'm not referring to these sophisticated offshore tax schemes – just simple straightforward tax planning.

The purpose of the book is to provide you with a logical and easy to follow process for organising, managing and optimising you financial affairs. It will also provide you with an insight into how a Chartered Financial Planner can help you create wealth, protect your wealth and then pass as much of your accumulated wealth to the next generation or to your chosen charities as possible.

I will explain the process and the technologies available to help you get improved investment returns, manage risk and structure your life tax-efficiently.

In simple terms, my aim is to make you money, save you money and save you time and hassle.

This is really important because most people either miss significant opportunities or, worse still, damage their own financial situation by attempting 'DIY' financial planning and wealth management. This approach is borne out of fear and ignorance. It is vitally important that you understand the value of taking professional advice and paying a fee to the planner so there is no vested interest in the sale of a product.

Red Adair famously said, "If you think a professional is expensive, wait 'til you try an amateur!"

The ideal outcome for me is a small book that is succinct, concise and easy to read. Having read the book, you will be provided with a simple, logical six-step process that will enable you to take full control of your financial affairs and understand the value of working with a professional. You will know what you can do to improve your own situation and how you should go about finding and working with a professional adviser - what questions should you ask?

This publication is for general information only and is not intended to be advice to any specific person. You are recommended to seek competent professional advice before taking or refraining from taking any action on the basis of the contents of this publication.

The Financial Conduct Authority (FCA) does not regulate tax advice, so this is outside the investment protection rules of the Financial Services and Markets Act and the Financial Services Compensation Scheme. This publication represents our understanding of law and HM Revenue & Customs practice as at 23/02/15.

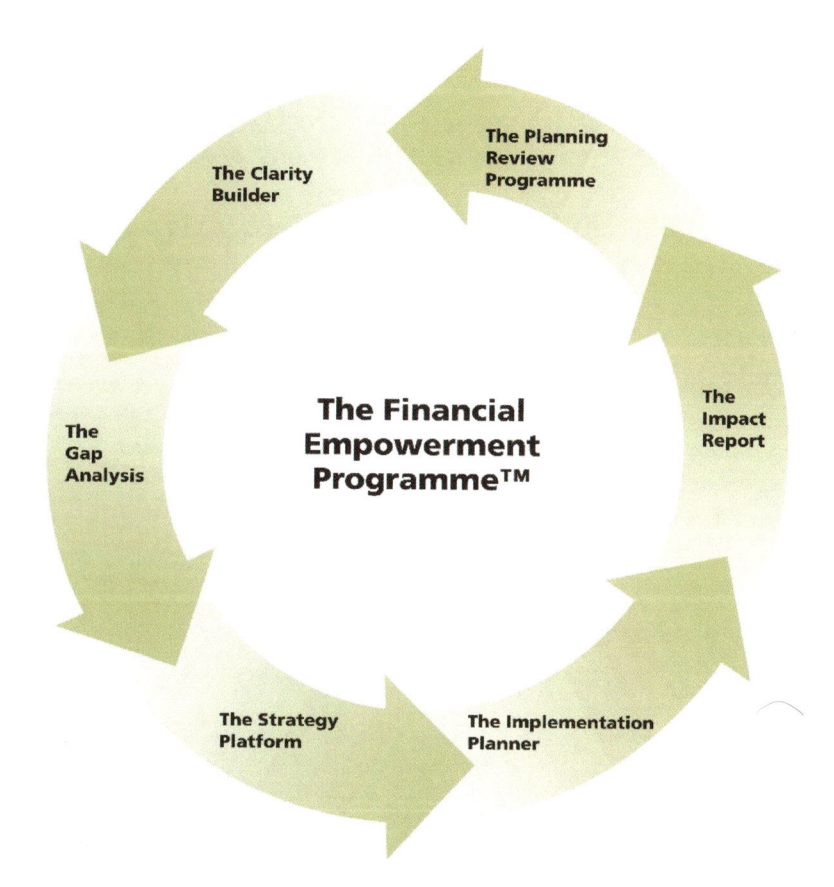

The Financial Empowerment Programme™

- The Clarity Builder
- The Planning Review Programme
- The Impact Report
- The Implementation Planner
- The Strategy Platform
- The Gap Analysis

The Exploratory Meeting

Many firms of Chartered Financial Planners will offer an exploratory meeting free of charge and without obligation.

This is your opportunity to find out about them and their business; and for them to start to get to know you. Take advantage of it.

I would go and meet them in their office because it provides you with the opportunity to meet the other team members and see how they operate. Also, remember that it is a two way process because it's as much about you weighing them up as it is them assessing whether they are the best firm to work with you.

It might give you an insight if I explained the five things that we look for in a prospective client. Incidentally, you will see that only one of the items relates to money:

To what extent would this person fully utilise the capabilities that we have in the practice?

What I mean by this is that we have a vast amount of technical competence in the team and very specialist knowledge in certain areas. There are certain areas that we do not major on. For example, we give very little advice on commercial mortgages – so we would serve the prospective client well by referring him or her on to a commercial finance specialist instead of us dealing with it in-house.

We would want to be sure that we are able to add value for the client and that we are operating within our scope of practice.

To what extent would this client enhance our proposition?

We are continually seeking ways in which we are able to enhance our client proposition and do things in a more efficient manner. We have found that clients are a very good source of ideas on how to improve what we do and how we do it.

An example of what I mean here is where a non-UK domiciled person approaches us as a client. Whilst we have the knowledge and expertise to advise non-UK domiciled clients, they may be domiciled in a jurisdiction that we haven't dealt with for some time. Consequently, it causes us to refresh our understanding and bring our technical knowledge right up-to-date. This brings it to the front of our minds and makes sure that the key technical facts are at our fingertips.

Will this person be a strong advocate for our business?

I realise that it is impossible for someone to recommend us until they have experienced the service and are entirely satisfied with the results. However, you can get a sense from people as to whether they are likely to want to develop a long-term relationship with us and whether they are likely to refer us on to their peers.

I sometimes say to people that we are like every other business in that our clients or customers are the lifeblood of our business; and that we are always seeking to build relationships with other people that would benefit from dealing with us. In other words, there has to be a certain amount of marketing activity going on; and the most cost effective way for us to grow our client bank is by referral and recommendation from an existing satisfied client.

That ultimately benefits the clients because the less time and money that we spend on acquiring new clients, the more time and money we have to invest in providing even better service to our existing clients. So it is a symbiotic relationship.

Is there a degree of rapport and are we going to enjoy the relationship?

It might surprise you to know that money is not the main motivator for most financial planners. It's accepted that a business has to make a profit in order to justify its existence and to create the cash resource necessary to invest in new capabilities, which benefits clients.

However, it is very important that we enjoy the relationship with a client. We want there to be a high level of trust and rapport between us.

Is this person capable of and willing to pay our fees?

This is the only monetary test for us. I know some firms set minimum thresholds in terms of investable assets or household income or even net worth, but we don't.

Your financial planner has to be paid. Good advice may not be cheap but it is always good value for money.

So that gives you a clue as to the type of questions that the financial planner will want answering at the exploratory meeting.

My suggestion is that you also give thought to the information that you would like to glean from the discussion and make sure you are fully prepared.

There should be some 'hard' facts and some 'soft' facts that you want to elicit. The hard facts are things such as the level of qualifications, the financial planning process, how investments are placed and managed and the fee structure.

The 'soft' facts will be issues such as whether there is rapport between you, how does the planner conduct himself, do you like their office environment, do they take the trouble to get to know you and find out what your aspirations are?

Prepare for this meeting by doing some background research about the adviser and the firm; their website is an obvious first port of call. Ask to see testimonials and copies of their marketing materials and their Client agreement and fee tariff for example. But also think about what it is that you want and what you don't want – think about past experiences that you have had with previous advisers and planners and consider the things that you valued and what you did not appreciate.

Form some questions in your mind before you go to the meeting.

I know, from a financial planners point of view, I really enjoy the exploratory meetings with people that ask incisive and insightful questions that demonstrate they have done some background research.

A good way to prepare is to ask yourself the following questions as a way of preparing for the meeting:

- What is your purpose for the meeting?
- Why is the meeting important to you?
- What is the ideal outcome for you?
- What are the specific things that you need to take away from the meeting for it to be successful?

Once you have decided to engage a particular financial planner, there are likely to be a series of steps to go through in the advice and implementation process. Each firm of planners will have their own approach.

The Financial Empowerment Programme™

In my mind there are six distinct steps in professional financial planning that have a logical progression.

Over the years, I have seen it all. I've had people walk into my office with shopping bags full of papers that represent their whole financial lives – wills, mortgages, pensions, investments; a lot of it in envelopes that haven't even been opened!

At the other end of the scale, I've met prospective clients that have their lives meticulously planned and recorded on spreadsheets and scanned onto memory sticks for us to simply import into our systems.

To be honest with you, I don't care how people have looked after their financial lives when they first come to see us; you might think it weird but there is a certain satisfaction in taking the shopping bags full of stuff, finding out what they've got and then presenting the client with a neat portfolio report showing them exactly what they have got. On the other hand, the person at the other end of the scale is nice to deal with because we can engage in the planning process much quicker; and its cheaper for the client, of course, because there is less work to do during the initial information gathering stages.

Wherever you are starting from, your financial planner will probably follow a logical process. I think the best way for me to articulate the process that you should follow, is to explain The Financial Empowerment Programme™ that we use at Matrix Capital Limited and that will be further explored as this book progresses:

Stage 1 - The Clarity Builder™

The Clarity Builder™ is designed to identify a client's aspirations and financial objectives. Also relevant personal and financial data is collected and planning assumptions are agreed. We then work with the client to gain an understanding of what is important to them and use Our First Conversation™ to identify the greatest **concerns** that need to be eliminated, the biggest **opportunities** to be focussed on and captured and the client's biggest **strengths** to be reinforced and maximised.

At the end of this stage the client receives a **Portfolio Report** that sets out accurate and up-to-date information on your existing arrangements and provides all the information necessary for our professional team to complete the next stage.

The big picture with Stage 1 of any financial planning process is to become very clear about what you've actually got at the moment and what it is that you want to achieve.

Stage 2 - The Gap Analysis™

During The Gap Analysis™ phase, our team of professionals process and analyse all of the information and data collected from all sources. Financial planning is both an art and a science; therefore attitudinal data gleaned from you forms an important part of this stage of the process.

A Snapshot Report™ is generated at the end of this stage showing projected outcomes measured against stated objectives. The report summarises any shortfall or over-provision within your current financial planning objectives. It assumes no changes are made to your current planning and therefore in simple terms provides you with a 'snapshot' of the future if you were to carry on as you are – highlighting areas for particular attention during the next stage.

Stage 3 - The Strategy Platform™

This is your bespoke personal financial plan, which outlines how to make most effective use of financial resources in order to meet your aspirations and objectives. At this stage our recommendations are presented generically as the objective is to provide a platform from which we are able to formulate and agree specific recommendations as to how your financial arrangements are structured now and in the future.

You will receive The Strategy Platform™ Report which is a bound Financial Plan incorporating detailed analysis and generic recommendations outlining the actions that need to be taken in order for you to reach your stated goals.

Stage 4 - The Implementation Planner™

This is the point at which the outline recommendations agreed at The Strategy Platform™ stage are translated into detailed recommendations covering specific investments, pension arrangements or protection products, which we will offer you from the whole of the market. It may also involve us working with your other advisers, such as your accountant or solicitor.

Detailed recommendations are presented to you and, subject to your agreement, any necessary documentation or instructions to third parties are completed at the **Implementation Meeting**. We will confirm specific recommendations made by us along with the rationale for each individual element of our advice. We will provide a clear explanation of the reasons why particular actions have been recommended and why they are suitable in the context of your agreed objectives. This will be embodied in the next stage of the process.

Stage 5 - The Impact Report™

This is a written report confirming the specific recommendations made by us at the Implementation Meeting. It documents and records the key elements of our advice, the rationale behind any advice and provides a clear explanation of the reasons why particular actions have been recommended and why they are suitable in the context of your agreed objectives.

The Impact Report™ demonstrates the effect that the implementation of specific recommendations has had on your financial plan. In other words you will know where you are, you will know what you want to achieve and know what remains to be done; highlighting what further work may be required from the team.

Stage 6 - The Planning Review Programme™

This stage recognises that effective financial planning is a continuous process and not a one-off event. Progress of your plan is reviewed (usually on an annual basis) and modified to take account of changes to your circumstances. This review provides an opportunity for you to reassess your aspirations and to review your financial plan in the light of performance and any changed circumstances.

The Matrix Capital team employs a powerful mix of mathematical reasoning and emotional understanding to ensure that you continue to receive the best possible service.

Following the review, Private Clients will receive a revised bound copy of The Strategy Platform™ Report reflecting any agreed amendments to your financial planning. Otherwise, a written summary of any issues arising from the review meeting will be provided.

The level of service provided is determined through discussion with you. Our aim is to reflect your particular needs and aspirations within the service provided.

So, there's an example of a financial planning process.

Your financial planner will need to go through a process; and there are key stages that you will need to be taken through as a client in order for you to receive robust advice:

- Information gathering
- Analysis
- Report and recommendations
- Implementation
- Confirming suitability and compliance
- On-going review and service

It will therefore save time and cost for you and make the process more valuable if you are properly prepared for your meetings and interactions with your financial planner. Knowing what the process is and what to expect at each stage will give you a great head start.

How to prepare for your initial meeting with your financial planner

Ignoring the exploratory meeting, most financial planners will need to meet with you at least twice where implementation is required. In my experience, particularly with more complex situations and where other professional advisers such as solicitors and accountants need to be involved, it can take 3-5 meetings.

The initial information-gathering meeting can be broken down in to three distinct areas, which are compliance and regulatory matters, hard data and 'soft' facts.

Every financial planner that is authorised and regulated by the Financial Conduct Authority (FCA) will be required to gather sufficient information to meet the 'Know your client' rules. They will also be required to undertake certain checks to enable them to satisfy the anti money-laundering regulations. They cannot make exceptions, even though they may know you very well and it may seem irrelevant in your particular circumstances.

The following is a checklist of the main items that you may wish to take to your initial meeting, or supply in advance of the meeting:

- Proof of identity – your current passport, driving licence and firearms certificate are examples
- Proof of address – your driving licence (if not already used for identity purposes) bank statement or utility bill, which have to be less than 3 months old
- Details of your existing savings and investments, including the amount invested, the current value and ownership
- Details of your existing pensions
- Details of loans and mortgages
- Details of any protection policies
- Details of any employee benefits available through your company or employer
- Assets and liabilities
- Income and expenditure
- Last will and testament and lasting powers of attorney
- Details of any trusts that you are a beneficiary of

These items will enable your financial planner to satisfy the regulatory requirements.

Chapter 1

Stage 1: The Clarity Builder™

Before you start the planning process, it is fundamental to have clarity about two issues.

The first is to have a clear vision as to where you want to end up and, secondly, it is vitally important to have a detailed understanding of your existing arrangements *before* taking any action.

This might seem a very obvious thing to say but having met with hundreds, if not thousands, of people in my professional life, it is amazing how many people fail to give these issues serious thought; many people that I have in mind when making that statement have been business owners and professional people that have very clear objectives for their companies and know exactly what resources are available to them, but have not applied the same thought process to their own personal circumstances.

Let's start to deal with the first issue of you beginning to become clear about what it is that you want to achieve in say the next three years, which is a good time-frame to consider.

A great question to ask yourself is, **"If we were meeting here 3 years from today, looking back over those years, what has to have happened both personally and professionally, during that period, for you to feel happy with your progress?** This is known as the *R-Factor Question*® which was created by Dan Sullivan of The Strategic Coach® based in Toronto, Canada.

We use this question as part of Our First Conversation™, right at the start of a relationship with clients and prospective clients. We have found that it really helps people to get clarity about what they actually want in life and what's important to them, which is crucially important for you in starting to create a financial plan.

You don't need to engage the services of a Chartered Financial Planner to find answers to that question; you can ask yourself that question, making sure you write down the answers. I suggest that you grab a pen and a piece of paper and start writing answers down, in no particular order, right now.

I'd also suggest that you do it on your own and get your spouse or partner to carry out the exercise as well and then discuss it. You may find that it is one of the most valuable conversations that you will have as a couple!

Don't think too deeply about the answers at this initial stage, just brainstorm it for now. You will fine-tune it and alter it as we progress.

You will notice that the question is structured in a particular way, in that it puts you in the perceptual position of having already achieved the outcomes and you're simply reviewing "what has happened". Without getting into a load of 'mind stuff', by imagining that you have already achieved whatever it is that you want, you are automatically visualising and checking how you feel about achieving it. That helps you to, first of all, make sure that it is actually what you want and, secondly, it helps you to attain it.

You will also notice that the question encourages you to focus on progress and not perfection, which is important for you staying out of the gap. Sorry, another bit of Dan Sullivan "speak"!

Let's just take a moment to explain what we mean by "staying out of the gap".
Essentially, most people have a habit of using their future aspirations as the point of reference to check progress. The problem with this strategy is that the goal is always slightly different to what you thought it would be when you originally set it. Your aim has probably expanded or moved further into the distance – that is, you are always mentally in the gap between where you are and where you want to be. Consequently, people never get the feeling of confidence and increased resourcefulness that flows from feeling success. Maintaining confidence and being highly resourceful are really important in achieving your goals

and aspirations – in other words, it is a bit of a chicken and egg situation.

So, to stay out of the "gap" my suggestion is that you always use the past as your point of reference when checking progress; and focus on progress and not perfection – you will make progress but you'll never achieve perfection. However, by staying out of the gap, you will achieve a lot more, faster and with greater significance.

Simple really, isn't it?

Once you've created your list, highlight the three most compelling aspirations – these become your personal goals for the next three years. Incidentally, I often have to explain to people that we don't want them to focus on financial or monetary aims – it's personal stuff that's important. The purpose of financial planning and wealth management is to support your personal aspirations and lifestyle goals; very few people in my experience choose to focus on monetary objectives – money is there to serve a purpose and to facilitate, not the goal itself.

The next step is to consider **three** vital pieces of information about you and your situation:

> What are the biggest **dangers** or concerns that need to be eliminated?

> What are the biggest **opportunities** to be focused on and captured?

> What are your biggest **strengths** to be reinforced and maximized?

Again, you need to brainstorm the answers to these questions and then highlight the three most important answers to each question – so you end up with a list of your three biggest concerns, your three biggest opportunities and your three biggest strengths.

This information is important because it determines in which direction you should aim and it identifies any immediate issues that need dealing with. It increases your level of confidence about the future and gives you clarity as to what capabilities and resources you have at your disposal that will help you get there. It will also give you a clue as to what outside capabilities and resources you need to find.

If you want to make life easy for yourself with these questions, go to our website:

http://www.matrixcapital.co.uk/our-first-conversation

Here you can download a copy of Our First Conversation™, which you can have with my compliments. It covers each of these questions and gives examples of the most common answers that people have given over the years. You will find it useful.

I'll let you into a little secret here.

If clients can't or won't answer the *R-Factor Question®* we will not take them on as clients. The main reason is that if someone does not have aspirations or won't articulate them, it is really difficult (if not impossible) to create a financial plan or give advice about how they should arrange their financial affairs and manage their wealth. Also, if I'm brutally honest with you, I get joy out of working with aspirational people; and I find it draining working with people that don't "come with batteries installed" so to speak.

Anyway, you now have the following information about yourself:

You are clear about the three really important things for you to achieve over the next three years – that could be, for example, to achieve early retirement or sell your business, become debt free, support your children through university or improve your health.
The biggest dangers or **concerns** have been identified – typical examples that I've heard over the years include, "I'm worried about what would happen to my family and my business if I died or fell seriously ill", "I don't have a plan" and "I don't have a clear understanding of what I've got – it needs someone to demystify things and explain it all to me in plain English."
You have worked out what the biggest **opportunities** are now and over the next three years – again, if it helps, examples of what people have said to me are, "franchise or sell my business", "take more time off without my income reducing" and "help my children get on to the property ladder and launch their careers."
Lastly, you have a better understanding of what you're really good at – your natural talents and your **strengths**. Examples of answers given by clients include, "strong marriage", "very good at planning and managing my time" and "growing a profitable business providing good personal income."

There you have it – the basis of a plan, which you can either start to create yourself or you can engage the services of a Chartered Financial Planner to help you. Whichever way you decide, you will have greater clarity about certain things:

- Your aims and aspirations – what is **really** important to you.
- The immediate **dangers** that need to be mitigated or ideally eliminated.
- What **opportunities** can be grasped – in other words, what's hot at the moment?
- How to utilise your **strengths** and natural talents to help you create a brighter and more significant future for you and your family.

The second part of gaining clarity is to have a detailed understanding of your existing financial arrangements, including your pensions, investments, mortgage, policies etc.

Many people that I meet seem to have accumulated a variety of financial products that they have purchased from a number of sources – banks, Independent Financial Adviser's (IFAs) and directly from providers. Often decisions to 'buy' these products were not part of a co-ordinated financial plan; rather it was because they were 'sold' the products by a financial adviser/salesman.

There are certain key pieces of information that you will need, which you should be able to find in the original documentation that you were presented with at the time that you established the financial product. If these documents are not readily available or you are unsure as to where to locate the detail, the simplest approach is to write directly to the product provider and ask for written confirmation.There are similar pieces of information that I would suggest you obtain on your investments, which might include Individual Savings Accounts (ISAs) investment bonds, unit trusts, and so on. Also, the same applies to any policies that you hold providing life cover, critical illness cover etc.

To be perfectly frank with you, once you've obtained this information, you are starting to get into the territory of needing professional advice.

Unless you have the ability to interpret the information, I would suggest that you sit down with your financial planner to at least make sure that you fully understand what you have got.

It is so easy to make assumptions or end up making decisions based upon incomplete information that put you in a worse financial position. For example, you don't want to cancel or cash in something without knowing exactly what you gain and what you lose by doing so. You can only make this type of decision once you have all of the information and you understand the consequences of your proposed action.

You now need to schedule out the key information on each of your existing arrangements in a way that allows you to keep a record and keep track of any changes. An Excel spreadsheet would be a way of doing this, but if you engage a financial planner, you would expect him or her to use specialist financial planning software that will keep track of all of your arrangements and be able to produce reports when required.

In summary, at the end of this first stage of the process, you know two very important bits of information:

- You know broadly what it is that you want to achieve, and;
- You have a clear understanding of what you have got.

The next step is The Gap Analysis™.

Chapter 2

Stage 2: The Gap Analysis™

The concept of this second stage is for you to establish what the gap is between where you are likely to end up assuming nothing changes and where you would like to get to as a result of this planning process.

Financial planning is both an art and a science. However, you can make it more scientific and therefore introduce precision into the calculations by adopting some reasoned and reasonable assumptions on factors, such as annual inflation rates, annual growth rates and interest rates.

You will also need to consider your income and expenditure requirements both now and into the future and also your assets and liabilities – now and in the future.

The aim is to create an accurate financial statement for yourself and your family at each of your key life stages in the future.

An important life stage, if you're not already retired, is retirement from your occupation, profession or your business.

So let's focus on retirement to illustrate the six key steps that you would need to undertake for this part of the financial planning process:

Step 1:
Calculate the net expenditure (in today's terms) required to meet your lifestyle requirements at your anticipated retirement age.

⬇

Step 2:
Calculate the net income that will be available (in today's terms) from your existing arrangements.

⬇

Step 3:
Calculate the shortfall in net income (in today's terms).

⬇

Step 4:
Calculate the shortfall in gross income (in today's terms).

⬇

Step 5:
Calculate the shortfall in gross income projected forwards to your anticipated retirement age.

⬇

Step 6:
Calculate the amount of income generating capital required to provide that shortfall in gross income.

Now let's consider the six steps in more detail; and give you some tools and tips with which to perform your own calculations:

Step 1: Calculate the net expenditure (in today's terms) required to meet your lifestyle requirements at your anticipated retirement age.

Prepare a schedule of your household expenditure as it stands now.

It is vital to know exactly what you spend your money on. Make sure that you list absolutely everything, leave no stone unturned in this process.

Include a contingency, because there is bound to be something that is missed.

A useful exercise to do for a limited period of time, a week or even a month, is to list on your smartphone or on paper every item of expenditure that you incur each day. Count how much money you take out with you each day and count it at night, then make sure that you are able to account for every penny. Go through your debit and credit card slips and make sure that you have included everything. Check your bank account and list out any cheques, standing orders, direct debits and BACS payments that have been made.

In other words, make sure that you know exactly what you do spend your money on; it is so easy to forget about incidental purchases that you make throughout the day.

Go through each item of expenditure and adjust the value as at your preferred retirement age, but make sure that you prepare the figures in today's terms for the time being.

Here are some examples of items of expenditure that are likely to reduce or disappear:

- School and university fees
- Travel and commuting to the office
- Income tax
- National Insurance contributions
- Mortgage repayments
- Endowments, ISA contributions and regular savings
- Insurance
- Child care
- Pension contributions
- HP and loans

Here are examples of items of expenditure that are likely to increase in retirement:

> Holidays
> Recreation and leisure
> Eating out
> Medical expenses and health insurance
> Opticians and dentistry
> Reading materials, music etc.
> Gifts and donations

This will provide you with a picture of your expenditure immediately after retirement.

Don't underestimate the work involved in this part of the process because if you are doing it properly it will provoke thought and conversation with your spouse as to what lifestyle you would really like in retirement. For instance, you may wish to do a lot of international travel or develop an interest that you've deferred such as golf or photography.

You are probably starting to understand why financial planning is considered to be both an art and a science because all of the calculations and planning is driven by the aspirations of you and your family.

In other words, you have to mentally take yourself to your retirement and start to visualise the lifestyle that you would like. Remember that it is probably not as far away as you might think. A 50 year old wanting to retire at 60 years has 120 months or to put in another way, 120 payslips from which to save!

For the purposes of this example, let's assume that you have worked out that your net annual expenditure post retirement is estimated to be £50,000 (a). Make a note of this because we are going to use it below.

Step 2: Calculate the net income that will be available (in today's terms) from your existing arrangements.

First start by calculating your anticipated gross income (in today's terms) from all sources, assuming nothing changes. You will then be able to estimate your available net income in today's terms by carrying out a simple income tax computation.

I would emphasise that you need to undertake this exercise on the basis that there are no changes made to either your circumstances or the level of investment currently being made. So, for example, if you are currently investing £1000 per month into your pension plan, make sure that you obtain projected income figures assuming that continues through to retirement.

The purpose of this stage in the planning process is to accurately assess the gap between where you will end up by continuing along the path you are currently following and where you would ideally like to arrive. One of the key reasons for approaching it in this manner is to provide you with the basis upon which to properly assess the viability of your goals and to have a better understanding of what needs to be done in order to achieve your aspirations.

To do this accurately, you will need to do some research. In particular, you will need to obtain an accurate projection of the gross income from each of your pensions, investments and assets that are specifically earmarked for retirement.

The following is a list of typical sources of future income:

- Your State Pension, the level of which you can find out by submitting a Form BR19. This form may be downloaded at http://www.direct.gov.uk/pdfs/state-pension-statement.pdf.
- Interest from deposit accounts and savings accounts.
- Withdrawals from investment bonds – 5% of the original investment may be withdrawn each year for 20 years without creating a 'chargeable event'.

- Anticipated annuities or incomes from your personal pension arrangements.
- Projected retirement income from past and present occupational pension schemes.
- On-going dividends and salaries from your business.
- Dividends from ISAs, unit trusts, open-ended investment companies (OEICs) investment trusts and shares.
- Rental income from properties.
- Consultancy fees and part-time employment.
- Non-taxable income/state benefits.
- Maintenance and other sources of income.

You may need to enlist the help of others to collate this information. For example, your financial planner or investment adviser should be able to provide projected incomes from pensions and investments. If you do not have access to either a financial planner or an investment adviser, the product providers themselves should be able to send you a projection.

Take care with the data because some of it will be in today's terms and some will be in tomorrow's terms. The important thing is to put all of the gross income on to the same basis.

My suggestion is that it is usually simpler to firstly put the gross income in to tomorrow's terms because most of the projected figures available from pension providers are expressed at the date of retirement. You can then bring the gross income figure into today's terms by using a very simple Present Value (PV) formula.

Either way, the figure that you need to arrive at is the anticipated gross income from all sources in today's terms.

So, for the purpose of this exercise, let's assume that you're total projected gross annual income from all sources at retirement is £75,000.

The next step is to bring that figure into today's terms by discounting it back using the annual rate at which you believe that your earnings will increase each year on average. Some planners use the National Average

Earnings Index, which you can obtain from the Office for National Statistics. However, my own view is that you should use your own assumptions because it varies so much depending upon your business or profession and where you are geographically.

This is the formula that we are now going to use to bring the Future Value (FV) of your anticipated gross annual income from all sources into today's terms (i.e. the Present Value (PV)):

$$PV = \frac{FV}{(1+r)^n}$$

Where:

PV = Present Value of your projected gross annual income
FV = Future Value of your projected gross annual income
r = Expected average annual increase in your gross annual income
n = Number of years between now and when your anticipate receiving the retirement income

Using your example, and assuming that you are 10 years from retirement and you expect your income to rise by and average of 5% per annum over the next 10 years, the calculation is as follows:

$$PV = \frac{£75,000}{(1+0.05)^{10}}$$

$$PV = \frac{£75,000}{1.343916379}$$

$$PV = £55,807$$

Now that we have the current value of your projected retirement income, you are able to estimate the projected net annual income in today's terms by preparing a simple tax computation.

You may wish to ask your financial planner or your accountant to prepare the tax computation for you; it does depend upon how accurate you want to be. But, remember to prepare the computation based upon you being retired but using present day tax rates and personal allowances. Also, remember that your National Insurance Contributions will stop if you are not going to be employed post retirement – so they need to be excluded.

To help you, this is the tax computation for a single person with a very simple set of circumstances retiring at age 60 years (2014/15) with pension income as their sole source of income:

Income Sources			Income
Employment			
Pension			£55,807.00
Total Employment			£55,807.00
Total Income			£55,807.00
Personal Allowance			£10,000
Taxable Income			£45,807.00
Tax	Income	Rate	£
On Non-savings Income			
Basic Rate	£31,865	20.0%	6,373.00
Upper Rate	£13,942	40.0%	5,576.80
Income Tax Liability	£46,367	(26.2%)	£11,949.80
Income Tax Payable			£11,949.80

Your projected net annual income in today's terms, using this example, is £55,807 - £11,950 = £43,857 (b)

33

Step 3: Calculate the shortfall in net income (in today's terms).

This step is very simple and straightforward.

Before we take the step though, it is worth understanding my point of view as to why I recommend that you do most of the planning in today's terms.

The other way to approach this is to project both the anticipated expenditure and the expected retirement income forwards to the date upon which you plan to retirement; and that would work because you are putting them both on the same basis.

However, by initially bringing income and expenditure back to today's values, I have found that clients find it easier to relate, because they know how much things cost now and we know what the various tax rates and allowances are at the moment. You know how much fuel costs at the moment but who knows what it will be in say 10 years time, we might even be driving vehicles powered by hydrogen by then!

Also, it is easier to adjust the calculations as things change, which means that each year closer to retirement, the figures should become increasingly more accurate and reflective of changes to your circumstances and the changes in legislation.

The shortfall in net income is simply the difference between your anticipated net income and your expected annual expenditure – in the example used:

Projected net annual income in today's terms (b)	£43,857
Minus net annual expenditure post retirement (a)	£50,000
Shortfall in net income in today's terms	£6,143

Step 4: Calculate the shortfall in gross income (in today's terms).

We now need to gross that figure back up again in today's terms by adding the tax that will be applicable.

This can be very simple or incredibly complicated depending upon how you approach this and where you are planning to receive the income from that is going to make up the shortfall – indeed it may come from a variety of sources.

For example, you may be taking a very simple approach of planning to increase your investments into your pension plan in which case the taxation of that income will be fairly straightforward. On the other hand, you may be planning to sell your business at retirement and withdraw income from an offshore trust and a range of other investments. You may also be planning to retire abroad and be subject to a different tax jurisdiction. The tax treatment will therefore vary considerably.

The more complex your circumstances, the greater the value that a financial planner is able to provide. You may also need to involve your accountant or tax adviser in working with your financial planner – a collaborative approach has huge benefits particularly where there is complexity.

Nevertheless, you need to arrive at the gross equivalent of your anticipated net income required to close the gap and help ensure that you have sufficient income with which to fund your lifestyle in retirement. You probably want to be 'elderly and comfortable' instead of 'old and broke'.

For a simple and straightforward situation, and to err on the side of caution, where you are going to be a higher rate taxpayer in retirement (40% for 2014/15) take the net shortfall, divide by 60 and multiply by 100.

Using the figures in our example, the additional gross income in today's that would be required to fully meet the shortfall is calculated as follows:

35

£6,143/60 x 100 = £10,238 per annum (gross)

Step 5: Calculate the shortfall in gross income projected forwards to your anticipated retirement age.

This is done by using the following formula:

$$FV = PV \times (1 + r)^n$$

FV = Future Value
PV = Present Value
r = annual rate of increase
n = number of years between now and retirement

Therefore, using our example of £10,238 as the gross annual income required to fill the gap, the calculation is as follows:

$FV = £10,238 \times (1 + 0.05)^{10}$

FV of gross income shortfall = **£16,677**

The key component of this equation is clearly the rate (n) that you adopt.

There is logic to using either RPI or CPI because they may more accurately reflect the increase in your cost of living that the income is seeking to keep pace with. However, you may wish to use a higher rate depending upon your own expectations.

If your income goes up at a faster rate than RPI or CPI, it is very possible that your standard of living will improve between now and retirement and your expectations at retirement may therefore be greater. The cautious approach would be to use the high rate for planning purposes.

Step 6: Calculate the amount of income generating capital required to provide that shortfall in gross income

The final step is to work out the amount of income generating capital or assets that are necessary to produce the shortfall of gross income at your anticipated retirement age. This will of course be the actual amount required at that time, not in today's terms.

You will note that I have not said anything about where that capital might come from; and I have purposely stayed away from suggesting a UK regulated pension at this point.

At this stage we are considering the concept of helping you to create sufficient financial independence to be able to run your life on 'unearned' income rather than 'earned' income, which is how you are likely to be living if you are not yet retired.

There are essentially four asset classes that have the potential to generate 'unearned' income; and what I mean by unearned income is income that comes to you whether you work or not. I realise that there is a technical tax distinction between 'earned' and 'unearned' but I've broadened the definition.

You probably go to work or run a business and get paid by way of salary, fees, bonuses or dividends from your own company shares. You will get to a point where you would like to be able to fund your chosen lifestyle irrespective of whether you work or not.

That will require you to have assets that have the capacity to generate income whether you work or run your business or not.

The four asset classes that I am alluding to are:

- Property – because it generates rental income.
- Equities (i.e. shares) – because they generate dividend income.
- Fixed Interest (e.g. gilts and corporate bonds) – because they generate interest.
- Cash – because it generates interest.

Whether these assets are accumulated by you acquiring them directly or wrapped up in some form of collective investment is a separate consideration. All you need to focus on at this stage is the overall amount of capital.

That said, in order to improve the accuracy of your calculations, you will need to make an assumption about the income yield that you use to determine the amount of capital required. The factors that you will need to consider (and this should also provoke a deep discussion about how you actually organise your assets and what you do with your business) are things such as:

- o   Will you be happy to amortise your capital in retirement to subsidise the 'income' requirement?
- o   Will you sell your business? If so, what is a realistic valuation?
- o   Do you prefer the tax efficiency of a traditional pension plan or would you favour a more flexible and more accessible investment vehicle?
- o   Are you expecting any inheritances?
- o   To what extent do you want to consider long-term care provision as part of your retirement income?
- o   Would you consider selling your home and trading down to release capital for retirement purposes?

These are the types of questions that will need to be considered as part of the detailed planning stage, which we call The Strategy Platform™.

A quick and simple (and lower risk) starting point for determining the amount of capital required is to assume that the capital will be accumulated in your pension fund and that an annuity will be purchased when you "crystallise" your fund – "crystallise" is the new term for taking benefits from your pension arrangements.

Now, we could get into a whole raft of possibilities including Purchased Life Annuities (PLAs) Capped Drawdown, Enhanced Annuities and so on. I would suggest that this is an area where you would benefit from independent advice. However, in the spirit of keeping it simple and to illustrate the process, I would suggest that you assume an annual income yield of 5% gross – you will be able to fine tune the planning at a later stage.

So, the equation is a very simple one now because you take the gross annual shortfall figure at retirement, divide it by 5 and multiply it by 100. Therefore, using the figures in the example, the amount of income generating capital that would be required to provide the gross annual income to fill the gap is:

£16,677/5 x 100 = £333,340

So, the additional amount of income generating capital you require to fully meet the gross income shortfall at your selected retirement age is **£333,340.**

The question now becomes, "what do I do with the information?"

You now have an understanding of the gap between where you are heading at the moment and where you would like to be.

You also have some idea of the size of the 'problem', if one exists at all because this exercise may have simply reassured you that there is no gap and that you are on track to achieve or exceed your retirement objectives. That in itself is valuable and may enable you to consider early retirement for example.

The other point that needs to be made is that I have only taken one area of financial planning to illustrate the process, which is retirement. You will have other issues that you may wish to address such as estate planning and inheritance tax management, or school fees planning, business succession, or long term care for example.

The Gap Analysis™ is designed to place you in a position where you make some broad decisions about whether you change your goals to make them more realistic or whether you leave them as they are and develop a plan to achieve them.

I would advise you to make sure that you fully explore all of the possibilities as to how you might achieve your goals, however ambitious they may appear. Again, this is where a professionally qualified financial planner would be able to help. It might require a degree of lateral thinking in order to come up with a plan that is viable.

Chapter 3

Stage 3: The Strategy Platform™

The purpose of this stage in the process is to create a working financial plan, ideally with a Lifetime cashflow forecast.

This is where you need to get down to the specifics because this creates the platform from which you will be able to make informed judgements about what you do towards achieving your goals.

You will probably need to engage with professional help to carry out this stage of the process; but nevertheless it will be helpful for you to understand the process in order for you to provide the information necessary for him or her to undertake this stage.

This is your bespoke personal financial plan, which outlines how to make most effective use of financial resources in order to meet your aspirations and objectives. At this stage your financial planner's recommendations are presented generically as the objective is to provide a platform from which we are able to formulate and agree specific recommendations as to how your financial arrangements are structured now and in the future.

You should receive **The Strategy Platform™ Report** which is a bound financial plan incorporating detailed analysis and generic recommendations outlining the actions that need to be taken in order for you to reach your stated goals.

This stage looks in detail at the key areas of financial planning, which would typically include the following:

1) Risk profile, including your attitude to risk.
2) Planning assumptions for capital appreciation, income yields etc.
3) Your '5 Dials'.
4) Your income tax computation.
5) Catastrophe analysis – family protection and ill-health needs analysis.

6) Your retirement plan.
7) Estate planning and inheritance tax computation.
8) Long-term care analysis.
9) School and university fees analysis.

Let's now consider each of these areas in turn.

1) Risk profile, including your attitude to risk.

Risk profiling is a large subject on its own; and there are varying opinions on how effective it is as a basis for investment planning and the approach that should be taken. However, I happen to believe that risk profiling and determining someone's attitude to risk are important starting points for a meaningful discussion on how someone's investments should be structured.

It is broken down into two areas of testing.

The first is an 'objective' test that considers:

- Your capacity for loss
- The time horizon for investment
- When you want to access the capital and/or income and
- How long you need the income and capital to last.

These are all important questions that need to be answered.

For example, if you intend accessing the capital within a very short period of time then it would point towards deposit based savings for your money because you want your capital to remain safe and you need quick access.

The second test is a 'subjective' one in that you are attempting to elicit how you feel about investment risk. I will discuss the subject of 'risk' later, but what is generally meant by risk is in fact 'volatility'. I often use the phrase, "let's make sure that your investments pass the 2am test" – in other words, you don't want sleepless nights if you hear on the news that the stock market has just suddenly dropped.

A word of warning here is to avoid 'pigeon-holing' yourself into a preordained risk profile. It is not an exact science, it is meant as a guide.

Also, the idea is to try and achieve the level of investment return that you need with your risk profile. There is no point taking additional risk if you don't need greater investment returns – you may be well advised to restructure your investment portfolio to reduce volatility and risk.

The other interesting thing that I have found is that you won't necessarily achieve a pro rata increase in investment returns as a result of exposing your investments to greater volatility and risk. There is a middle ground where respectable long-term returns may be achieved without taking undue risk.

Don't assume that you will achieve a greater return as a result of taking greater risk.

2) Planning Assumptions

This has been covered under The Gap Analysis™.

However, the issue at this stage is that you need to make a decision about the assumptions that are going to be used for planning purposes. They need to be both reasoned and reasonable.

Opinion will vary but you do need to make some assumptions in order to bring precision and accuracy into the planning. A financial planner will have specialist software that will enable you to change the assumptions on the hoof and show the changes to the projected outcomes to your financial plan.

If you are doing this for yourself, I would suggest that you set up your spreadsheet with formulae that allow you to change assumptions on such things as capital growth, income yields, price inflation and earnings inflation. This will allow you to change the assumptions and very quickly see the impact upon the projected outcomes.

3) Your '5 Dials'

The 5 Dials is an analogy taken from the world of an airline pilot and is one of Dan Sullivan's concepts.

You will have seen that a pilot of an aircraft has a myriad of dials in the cockpit; and you may have wondered how on earth the pilot monitors all of those dials in order to make sure that the plane takes off and lands properly.

The answer is that, they don't monitor them all – they only monitor five.

If there is an irregular reading on a particular dial, there is a bank of dials below that the pilot will then look at, and so on until the specific problem has been identified.

I suggest that you take this approach with your own financial planning and wealth management. In other words, decide on the 5 most important numbers to monitor that would tell you instantly if something was off course with your financial life.

If you run a business, you will already be familiar with this concept – the directors or partners of a business would decide upon which key performance indicators to monitor that give them an ongoing and up-to-date read out on the health of the company. For example, they might look at cash on the balance sheet, total revenue, operating profit per employee and price/earnings (P/E) ratio. If one or more of these numbers is under or over budget, it causes the directors or partners to look more closely at what is going on in their business.

If the total revenue has dropped, the directors would probably want to know how the sales are broken down across the product range, individual customers and geographically to try and pinpoint where sales have dipped. They would then drill down to specific customers and sales team members to identify and rectify the problem.

Without monitoring that first 'dial' the business owner would have no idea where to look to identify the specific problem and take corrective action. The same applies in your own personal financial life.

I'm not suggesting for one moment that you run your life like a business; I said at the start that money is not the goal; it is simply an enabler for you. The best things in life are free, but it usually costs money to either provide the freedom to not do the things you loath or the freedom to do the things you love.

So, what are the '5 Dials' that you should be monitoring?

The answer is that you should decide that for yourself. However, I can give you a few ideas to think about.

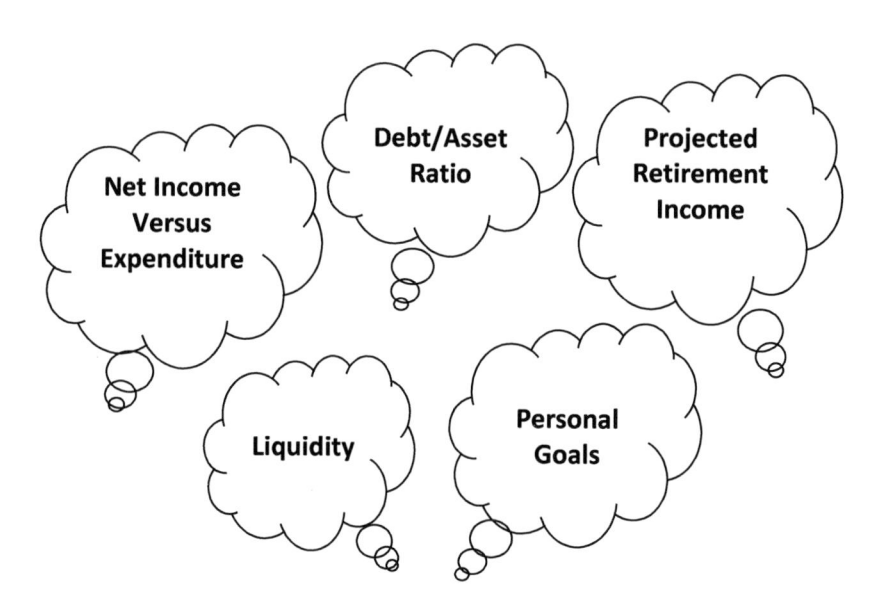

- Net Income Versus Expenditure
- Debt/Asset Ratio
- Projected Retirement Income
- Liquidity
- Personal Goals

Dial 1: Liquidity

In my view, it is very important for people to make sure that they have access to cash that they can get their hands on at a moment's notice.

There are some very sound reasons why you should monitor your own personal liquidity:

What happens if an emergency occurs? It could be something as simple as the car breaks down and you're faced with a repair bill. It could also be something more costly. You may not want to, or be able to, resort to borrowing to cover the sudden cost.

You may have a known purchase coming up in the near future. For example, a holiday or improvements to the home.

People with a greater appetite for risk, particularly business owners, sometimes need cash to take advantage of an opportunity that suddenly presents itself; conversely, they may have taken a chance on something that has gone wrong and they need cash to dig themselves out of a financial hole.

If your asset backed investments, which you set up for long-term growth, suddenly drop in value, it may not be to your advantage to cash in the investment but leave it intact until markets have moved in a positive direction. In other words, you can meet your needs from your cash and leave your investments alone for a while. Having a cash resource in these circumstances can save you £1000s in the long run.

If you are relying upon your pension plan to provide income from a certain retirement date, and the markets have fallen just before you 'crystallise' your benefits, having cash to tide you over can be a Godsend.

The amount really depends upon your circumstances; but a guide would be to add up the amount of cash that you require for known items of expenditure over, say, the next 3 years. Then add a buffer for emergencies together with a minimum 3 months net income. This amount of money should then be placed on deposit with a bank or building society at the best rates that you can find.

If you intend to deposit more than £85,000 be aware of the Financial Services Compensation Scheme (FSCS) compensation limits, which were set at £85,000 per person per banking group from 31st December 2010. You may wish to spread the cash between banking groups. Make sure that the banks are in fact in different groups because Lloyds Bank, as an example, includes Lloyds Bank itself, Halifax, Bank of Scotland and Birmingham Midshires. There are a number of other examples.

You should also consider spreading the funds between spouses for the same reason, but also there may be a tax advantage if you and your spouse are paying different rates of income tax.

Dial 2: Net income-v-expenditure

Are you spending more or less than your net income?

If you are spending more that your net income, either your cash reserve is being depleted or your debts are rising. If your debts are rising, it means that your expenditure is going to have to rise in future or you're going to have to release cash by selling something at some point.

If you are spending less than your net income, what are you doing with the surplus?

Should you be using that surplus to pay down debt or to turn it into capital? If you pay down debt, which debt should you pay off first? Should you put the surplus into cash to improve your liquidity? Should you make a contribution to your pension? If so, whose pension plan do you invest it in?

There are a whole host of questions for you to answer and options for you to consider. Whether you address these issues yourself or whether you seek professional guidance, is up to you. I would, of course, suggest that you seek advice because it will pay dividends in the long run.

So, it is critical that you know where you are with your income and expenditure and, the easiest way of doing this is to prepare a budget.

If you were engaging a firm such as ours, you would end up with a detailed report showing both numerically and graphically where your money comes from and where it goes.

A pie chart of your income and expenditure has value as well as the numbers because it gives you an overview and helps you to think strategically. For example, if it shows that you are spending more on tax and National Insurance Contributions, it might cause you to consider redistributing income between you and your spouse, if that option is available to you. Or it might, for example, lead on to you having a conversation with your financial planner and accountant about restructuring the remuneration from your business.

The point is that unless you know how your income and expenditure interact, you are missing out on the opportunity of improving your overall financial well-being.

Dial 3: Debt/Asset ratio

To use another business analogy, what is your 'gearing' like?

Are you debt free or are your debts equal to 100% of your assets, or are you somewhere in between?

Occasionally, I'll get someone come into my office seeking advice on areas such as retirement planning or inheritance tax planning; but when we schedule out their assets and liabilities, we see that they are very highly geared. In other words, their debts are a high proportion of their assets.

Of course it's your money and it's your life, so you make your own decision about how you prioritise things. However, my suggestion in these circumstances is invariably for them to apply surplus income or capital to the reduction of debt and liabilities before they consider making long-term investments.

The main reason for this is that if something were to go wrong, which could be poor health, death, and loss of employment – it may create financial hardship for you and your family if you or your spouse is left with debts that cannot be serviced.

My suggestion is that you schedule out all of your assets and all of your liabilities. Be objective and be entirely honest and accurate.

> Example:
>
> Total liabilities: £357,000
> Total assets: £565,000
> £357,000/£565,000 x 100%
> = 63% gearing.

I suggest that if this rises above 75%, you need to look more closely and take steps to improve the ratio.

Dial 4: Projected retirement income

Almost everyone on this planet runs their lifestyle based upon 'earned' income whilst they are working or actively running their business. At some point, most people want to be able to live their lives using 'unearned' income that comes in irrespective of whether they are working or not.

I realise that the financial professionals reading this might argue with me that income such as dividends are technically 'unearned' income and that a lot of Company Directors choose to take dividends in preference to salary or bonus; but what I'm referring to is income that does not rely on your ability to work or run your business.

In order to create this type of income, you need capital assets that generate income – it's not rocket science. By way of a reminder, the four main asset classes that generate income are as described above:

- Cash – because it produces interest.
- Property – because it produces rent.
- Shares – because they produce dividends.
- Fixed interest (e.g. Government Gilts and Corporate Bonds) – because they produce interest, or what is called a 'coupon'.

Where you accumulate those assets and in what proportion, and in whose ownership are different questions. Unless you have specialist knowledge, this is where you are very likely to need the services of a competent adviser.

I remember sitting next to a very successful entrepreneur at a formal dinner in London some years ago. I knew he was a multi-millionaire, so I asked him, "How do you become a multi-millionaire?"

He asked me if I was genuinely interested, which surprised me but I said I was, so he proceeded to tell me.

He said, first of all make sure that you are living within your means and spending less than you are earning. The next step was to convert the surplus income into capital, but a certain type of capital – capital that generates income; all of the assets mentioned above, in fact.

His advice was to also reinvest the income generated from the capital into more capital, whilst at the same time buying more capital with your surplus income. Work smart to increase the amount of surplus income so that you can create more income producing capital.

Eventually, you get to the point where the income from the capital at least equals the income from your job or business, which means that you've achieved financial independence. Becoming a multi-millionaire is then simply about continuing the journey until your capital is greater than £2m!

Simple, eh?

Whether you call it retirement income or just getting to the position in life where you can choose to work or not is not the point. What is important is that you monitor your projected future income that you expect to receive when you decide not to work or retire from your business.

Once you know how much capital you will need, you can then deduct the amount of capital (e.g. pension, investments, assets etc.) that you have now and arrive at the shortfall.

Once you know that number, you can then work out how much you need to save, monthly annually or as a lump sum.

Where you invest the money to accumulate the required capital is as I say an area where you are likely to need to take professional advice on.

Dial 5: Personal Goals

I put this last to highlight the point that this is the reason why you should be interested in making sure that your financial planning is well organised and regularly reviewed.

You've heard the clichés, but it is true that this is not a practice run; unless you believe in reincarnation, this is **your** life and why not have the lifestyle that you and your family desire?

Your personal and family aspirations give meaning to your plan; they are the purpose behind the process.

Having spent many years, and a lot of money, trying to distil my thinking down to what I want down to the pure essence of my desires, I have settled on the thought that what I'm really pursuing is 'happiness'.

But then, you ask the question, "What would make me happy?"

One way to answer that is to say that it is 'freedom' that provides happiness; and that usually means freedom away from something and/or freedom towards something. For example, you may desire freedom from being tied to your business and freedom to spend more time with your children and family.

The R-Factor Question® that I wrote about earlier is one way of approaching the issue of becoming clear about your goals and aspirations. Another way is to consider what you value – in other words, what are your personal values. Once you're clear about your values, you should be able to decide which goals to set for you and your family.

Many years ago, I attended a seminar and the speaker asked us to take out a piece of paper and quickly write down the answers to the following questions. You might like to do the same:

> *If you knew that you were going to die in 3 years time, what are the 3 most important things that you would do?*
>
> *If you had been diagnosed with cancer and the prognosis was 3 months, what are the 3 most important things you would do?*
>
> *If you were on a plane, which was hurtling to the ground and you had about 3 minutes before the crash, what is the one thing that you would do?*
>
> *If you're anything like me, whenever I do this type of exercise, health and relationships are always the top two answers.*

Just as an aside, because it happens to be topical with me, let me ask a question that I've asked myself: if health and relationships are number 1, why is it that they are not the focus of our daily lives? Why do we take it for granted that we will remain healthy and good relationships with people close to us will continue regardless? Why do we focus on other things in our daily lives like business, clients, cash flow management, recruitment, the news and so?

Years ago, I used to use the phrase; "The fridge never lies". This was because I used to put pictures of the things I desired on the fridge door in the belief that continually visualising those things would cause my unconscious minds to direct me to take the actions that were necessary to bring them into reality. It's amazing how many of those things have actually come to fruition over the years.

Whichever way you deal with the issue of becoming clear about your goals doesn't really matter. What does matter is that you have a clear understanding of what it is that you're planning for: a plan without a goal is pointless and a goal without a plan will probably mean that it takes longer to achieve, if at all.

So, gain clarity about your goals and write them down – share them with your spouse, better still, do the exercise together.

Once you have your goals and when you want to achieve them, you can work out what the financial aspect to those goals is. In other words, how much money will it cost and when do you need the money?

You will then start to revisit your income and expenditure and your assets and liabilities with a new perspective. You will probably start to notice items of expenditure that could be diverted into funding what's really important to you. For example, you may decide that you are spending too much on eating out and you don't have enough being saved for a nice family holiday.

By sorting out your important aspirations and knowing in detail what your income and expenditure is and what assets and liabilities you have, you have created a platform for making informed judgements about what you do with your money.

I remember years ago, I had a Jewish client; and when I first met him, he pulled out a wodge of building society passbooks and went on to explain what each one was for. He had one each for his sons' bar mitzvahs and his daughter's wedding. It's a bit like my grandmother who used to have tea caddies for different things – she had one for the rent and one for groceries and one for pocket money for the grand kids, which was always my favourite!

It might seem old fashioned but it's a mind-set that does keep you focussed on organising your income and expenditure and making sure that it is aligned with what's important to you.

4) Your Income Tax Computation

Some of the financial planning reasons why you would want an accurate tax computation are as follows:

- o To identify any planning opportunities that arise from different rates of income tax and capital gains tax between spouses.
- o To identify any opportunities for restructuring your remuneration, which is particularly relevant to shareholding directors who are able to pay themselves dividends and bonuses.
- o To decide whether to invest in your pension fund this year and, if so, to calculate the tax consequences.
- o To decide whether to change the ownership of assets before disposal to ensure that you fully utilise each spouses CGT Allowances and basic rate tax slice.
- o To make decisions on tax beneficial investments (e.g. EIS, VCT and BPRA) and whether to use Gift Aid to help mitigate income tax at the highest rate for the household.

Whether you carry out your own tax computation or whether you engage a professional adviser to undertake the task is your choice, but I would encourage you to prepare accurate figures well before the end of the tax year (i.e. 5th April) and before the end of the current accounting period if you run a business.

An accountant is generally only interested in preparing a tax computation after the event when all of the figures are known. However, it is extremely difficult, if not impossible to, take advantage of a wide range of tax planning and financial planning opportunities after the year-end as expired.

If you engage a financial planner, they should be expected to work in collaboration with your accountant and tax adviser to make sure that you take advantage of as many opportunities as possible. From a professional point of view, I'm always disappointed when I come across missed opportunities that have been created simply because the financial planner and the accountant didn't talk to each other early enough.

5) Catastrophe analysis – what happens in the event of sudden death or serious illness?

Life never goes to plan and sometimes events can occur out of the blue that dramatically change everything.

This could be as a result of death of a spouse, a serious illness or disability or sudden loss of income because your business fails or through redundancy.

Whilst it may be tempting to gloss over this issue on the basis that you don't want to consider such a negative situation or you prefer to take a chance on one of those situations not occurring, I would encourage you to grasp the nettle and prepare a needs analysis for each situation.

The Gap Analysis™ gives you a broad understanding as to whether there is a shortfall but the idea at this stage is to bring precision into the calculations and start to formulate a contingency plan to deal with the situation should it arise in the future.

The Gap Analysis™ provides you with an understanding as to what would happen, assuming nothing changes. You now need to become very clear as to what you would want to happen should you either die unexpectedly of suffer a serious illness or disability (e.g. heart attack, stroke or major accident). This should provoke a discussion with your spouse and with your business partners.

It's important to consider the impact upon your business as well as your family. You may be in business with your spouse and children, which adds another dimension.

In any event, if you are relying upon either the capital value of your equity in the business or the continuing income stream to help support your spouse and family in the event of your death or serious illness, you will need to consider what would actually happen to the business and the value of your equity in that business in those circumstances.

A question that I often ask business owners when I meet them in their office, is whether they have insured their desk against theft or destruction. The answer they give is invariably that it is insured. I then ask whether the person sat behind the desk is also insured. Probably 90% of the time, the answer is "no".

Doesn't it strike you as odd that the business would insure a piece of furniture that would have little impact upon the business if it went missing but not insure a person in the business, whose disappearance even for a few months, would have a hugely detrimental effect on the operation of the business?

6) Your Retirement Plan

If we consider the calculation that we undertook in Chapter 2, the example showed that **£333,340** was required at aged 60 years in order to generate the gross income to fully plug the retirement income gap.

The next question to consider is how you might plan to accumulate the amount of additional capital that you require in retirement?

Saving lump sums and making regular contributions into your pension plan are obvious options, which offer very attractive tax incentives at outset. However, there is a range of other options that you may wish to consider, which include:

- Building up savings in ISAs, unit trusts, OEICs and deposit accounts.
- Using the net proceeds from the sale of your business.
- Planning to trade down from your main residence to release capital for reinvestment.
- Utilising expected legacies and inheritances.
- Regular savings plans such as maximum investment plans

Whichever option (or range of options) you decide, if you intend making regular contributions, you will need to calculate how much you will need to save into order to build up a capital sum of sufficient size at retirement.

7) Estate Planning and Inheritance Tax Computation

It has been said that inheritance tax (IHT) is a tax of choice.

This might seem an outlandish claim, but there is in fact a lot of truth to the statement. This is because it is possible, with careful planning, to organise your estate in such a way that it is below the Nil Rate band upon death. A quick example would be someone who has willed his or her entire estate to a registered charity, such as the National Trust; in which case the estate would pass without creating an inheritance tax charge.

The first port of call is always to calculate the liability to IHT on the assumption that both of you (if you are a couple) died last night. A basic template is as follows:

Assets	£
Main residence	
Holiday home/Other properties	
Commercial properties	
Agricultural land	
Cars, boat etc.	
Household contents	
Bank and building society deposit accounts	
Investments (stocks and shares, bonds, ISAs etc.)	
Life assurance policies (if not in trust)	
Pension lump sum (if not in trust)	
Other assets	
Non-exempt gifts made within the last 7 years	
Total value of assets	
Less liabilities	
Mortgages	
Loans, hire purchase, credit cards	
Funeral expenses	
Other liabilities (e.g. unpaid tax)	
Total liabilities	
Less reliefs (e.g. Business Property Relief or Agricultural Relief)	
Net value of estate	
Less Nil Rate Band	
Less Transferrable Nil Rate Band	
Taxable value of estate	
Tax at 40%	
Less Taper relief	
IHT payable upon the death of both	

If either you or your spouse have been widowed, there may be a transferrable nil rate band available from the previous deceased spouse's estate. However, the rules only allow you to use a maximum of two nil rate bands. So, if you are in this situation, you should seek advice on utilising the additional nil rate band by for example establishing a nil rate band discretionary trust within the wording of your wills.

This is very important because without careful planning, a nil rate band of £325,000 (2014/15) may be lost resulting in the IHT liability being £130,000 higher than it would otherwise have been.

Estate planning is one area in particular where the best results are obtained with your financial planner working in collaboration with a solicitor and possibly an accountant, where there are business and/or agricultural assets to consider.

Chapter 4

Stage 4: The Implementation Planner™

This is where the financial plan is implemented.

There is a whole range of areas where advice and implementation may be required. Some of these areas are:

- Re-balancing your investment portfolio in accordance with your current risk profile and investment objectives.
- Establishing a last will and testament and setting up trusts.
- Fund switching
- Transferring pensions, ISAs and collective investments
- Establishing a co-shareholder or partnership agreement
- Key person or key director protection
- Changing the structure of ownership to mitigate inheritance tax

It is highly likely at this stage that you will need to engage a professional financial planner who is authorised by The Financial Conduct Authority (FCA). The key reason for this is that many areas require advice on the establishment of financial products that are regulated by the FCA, and only those with the 'permissions' granted by the FCA may deal with many of the investments and pensions that you may need.

You could deal directly with individual insurance companies and product providers but you would need the ability to be able to properly identify which financial product your investments are most suitable – otherwise, you are groping in the dark.

Whilst it may be possible for you to establish your own financial arrangements directly with investment companies and product providers, for all practical purposes, you are well advised to engage someone that has the relevant authorisations and competences to deal with your circumstances.

The other thing to bear in mind is that if you don't require advice, the product provider or investment house is really being asked by you to effect the transaction on an 'execution only' basis. The consequences of this are that you have no guarantee that the product or investment is suitable and the product provider cannot be held responsible if it subsequently transpires that it wasn't suitable. In other words, you take full responsibility.

If a product or investment has been arranged for you on an 'advisory' basis by an appropriately authorised adviser, you will have recourse to that adviser.

I have no hesitation in urging you to seek professional advice from a suitably qualified adviser that is authorised and regulated by the FCA.

The question then becomes, how do you go about finding and engaging the right firm of advisers for you.

Choosing the right adviser

I've learned from experience (and it cost me a lot to learn the lesson) that you need to be careful when choosing a professional adviser.

But, so as to not put the cart before the horse, let's consider why you might want to engage a professional financial planner and financial adviser in the first place?

I will then explain the different types of planner and adviser operating in the market place; the questions that you should ask and the rationale for you paying a fee rather than the adviser being paid by commissions or payments from product providers.

I suppose the first key question is what can a professional financial planner do for you that you can't do for yourself?

I'll attempt to answer that question from the point of view of the problems that I have seen encountered by people using the DIY approach. Broadly, the problems are:

You may be well intended and motivated at the start, but the reality is that you probably won't actually get around to getting the job done.

I can hear you say, "that does not apply to me" and maybe you are correct, but in my experience very few people do it under their own steam.

I accept that some people have created so much wealth that they never have to worry about financial security but if you are in the wealth creation phase of your life, you'll reach a point of financial security much quicker and with less risk if you have a plan. Alternatively, if you have already created significant wealth, you are likely to want to ensure that your wealth is protected and passed on in the most appropriate manner to the individuals and organisations that you have decided to pass your accumulated wealth to.

If you are paying a financial planner to prepare a financial plan and give advice, they will get the job done because that is their business and you won't pay them until they have completed the task.

There is a danger of you having a lack of objectivity about your own circumstances and objectives.

A professional adviser will be very skilled at asking succinct questions that not only establish the 'hard' facts but also elicit the 'soft' facts such as your attitude to risk and how you prioritise your objectives.

There aren't many people with the financial wherewithal to understand the technicalities of financial products such as pensions and investments; and how to create finance projections based upon reasoned and reasonable assumptions on factors such as annual inflation rates and annuity rates.

A Chartered Financial Planner has all of that knowledge and experience at their fingertips. They also have access to software and technology to achieve a level of precision with the numbers that you are unlikely to achieve.

With a lot of research and effort, you may be able to design your own house and draw up plans that will pass Building Control, obtain Planning Permission and get built. However, I would suggest that a Chartered Architect would create a better result, faster and more cost effectively – that's the value of taking professional advice.

I can give you countless examples of situations where people have come into our office after taking advice from an unqualified adviser or having taken the DIY approach. It gives me no pleasure to see people that are in a far worse financial position than they need have been through their own ignorance or through the ineptitude of an unqualified person.

One slightly embarrassing situation for me was a couple that came to see me; I commented that the investment performance was shockingly bad on the husband's self-invested personal pension (SIPP) and suggested that the investment adviser should be taken to task – the wife started to giggle and the husband blushed. It transpired that the husband had been doing his own investment management. Oops!

Another more serious example was four company directors who had had all their pensions transferred by a previous adviser. When we analysed what had happened, we discovered that the previous adviser had unwittingly reduced the amount of tax free cash that two of the directors were entitled to, which would have cost them £100,000s in the long term. Fortunately, we managed to persuade the pension provider to unravel the mistake and put the client back into the position they were in before the transfer took place, which incidentally did the previous adviser a huge favour in that they avoided a costly negligence claim.

Where can you go for advice and what are your options?

On 1st January 2013, the Financial Services Authority (now called the Financial Conduct Authority (FCA)) which is the regulator for financial planners, investment advisers and intermediaries, implemented a new set of rules. These included a higher qualification level for financial planners and investment advisers and the banning of commission payments for the sale of investment and pension products.

They also polarised advice between 'independent' and 'restricted'.

These changes may have gone unnoticed by some members of the general public but are significant changes that people need to understand.

1) Qualifications

In order for an adviser or planner to give advice on investments and pensions, the FCA must be satisfied that the individual has at least achieved a relevant QCA Level 4 (i.e. Diploma) qualification. This is roughly equivalent to the first year of a university BSc or BA degree course.

Let me ask you a question...

If you were sat in your doctor's surgery and he or she divulged that they had only completed the first year of medical school, would you follow their advice?

The answer is probably "no" because you would expect your GP to be fully qualified and competent to give robust advice; and that means you would expect them to have at least attained a degree in medicine, which is QCA Level 6.

In the world of financial planning, investment advice and wealth management, that means that the adviser or planner with a relevant university degree level qualification (QCA Level 6) would be a Chartered Financial Planner. There is a place for financial planners and advisers that are not Chartered; most firms of Chartered Accountants for example have unqualified accountants working on client files and they do a great job within their scope of practice. Also, it is true to say that there are many financial advisers and financial planners who are not yet Chartered but do an excellent job and often have specialist knowledge that a 'general practitioner' would not have.

Being 'Chartered' is not the be all and end all, but it does provide reassurance that the adviser you are dealing with has demonstrated a high level of technical knowledge and adherence to a strict code of conduct.

There are other advisers that are involved in financial planning, investment advice and wealth management; and they include accountants, solicitors, bankers, stockbrokers, pension scheme administrators and discretionary fund managers. However, I would contend that it is only the Chartered Financial Planner, authorised by the FCA, who is qualified to provide holistic financial planning, investment advice and a comprehensive wealth management service to clients.

Your financial planner sits alongside you as the client; he or she is the only person that will fully understand the client's circumstances, their aspirations and their feelings and attitudes. This means that the financial planner is best placed to co-ordinate the implementation of the plan with other professionals.

Also, you need to be careful as to who you take advice from. For example, it is unlikely that your accountant and solicitor are authorised to provide investment and pension advice; but many people seem to go to these professionals for this type of advice. Make sure that the person from whom you are seeking advice is operating within their scope of practice.

So, when selecting which financial planner, financial adviser or investment adviser to engage, the first thing to establish is their level of professional qualifications – ideally they should be Chartered Financial Planners. They will either have APFS or FPFS as designatory letters after their name, depending upon whether they are an Associate of the Personal Finance Society (PFS) or a Fellow.

The Personal Finance Society is the main professional body for financial services professionals in the UK, with over 35,000 members at the time of writing; and responsible for issuing Statements of Professional Standing (SPS) which every practicing adviser must hold in order to give advice. It is therefore a good idea to check that the financial planner or financial adviser that you are dealing with holds a valid SPS.

Bear in mind though that the SPS only confirms that the adviser or planner has complied with minimum standards; it does not mean they are Chartered Financial Planners – you will need to check this out by referring to their designatory letters or ask to see the actual certificate, which they will probably have on display in their office.

2) Independent or restricted advice?

The next thing to consider when choosing a professional adviser is whether they are "independent" or "restricted"?

If a financial adviser or financial planner declares themselves to be an 'independent' adviser, they will need to consider a broader range of products for their clients. They will need to provide unbiased, unrestricted advice based on a comprehensive and fair analysis of the relevant market; and all advisers will have to inform their clients, before providing advice, whether they provide 'independent' or 'restricted' advice'.

The key points to note are:

Whether a firm decides to offer Independent or Restricted advice, the same requirements regarding qualifications and adviser charging will apply to that firm and its advisers.

It is the **firm** that actually provides the advice to the client, which could be Independent or Restricted, or both.

A key question to ask when determining status is whether a firm **cannot** or **will not** ever recommend a product type or a product provider, even if that product or that product provider would be suitable for a client.

Independence refers to the activity **'Advising on Packaged Products'** (to be 'Retail Investment Products' from 31st December 2012). A Retail

Investment Adviser will not need to advise on **Securities** or **Derivatives** in order to hold themselves out as Independent.

Stock-broking and wealth management firms advising retail clients on retail investment products such as Exchange Traded Funds (ETFs) Structured Capital at Risk or Unregulated Collective Investment Schemes (UCIS) will be drawn into the same regulatory regime as the financial adviser. This means that they too will be subject to the requirements for Level 4 qualifications, Independence and Adviser Charging.

2a) Independent

An independent financial adviser (IFA) must consider all the options open to their clients—all the products offered by all the investment providers. This part of RDR is designed to ensure that individuals receive advice that is 100% unbiased and wholly in their best interests.

But does independent always mean independent? This is where it can get a little confusing.

If a financial adviser finds that a certain group of clients has specific investment needs and objectives that would be met by a *relevant* portion of the overall market, such as ethical investments, they can focus on this area alone and still call their advice 'independent' within that particular market, as long as they consider all ethical investment products and all ethical investment providers. However, the firm cannot hold itself out as an "independent financial advice" (IFA) firm, because this would imply that it advises on more than just ethical investment options.

What is deemed a *relevant* portion of the market is set by you the client and not by the adviser. If a client indicates that they are only interested in ethical and socially responsible investments, it is clear that there is a range of products that would never be suitable for them, namely non-ethical investments. This means that the adviser would not need to consider these products when forming independent advice for the client.

To be clear, a hypothetical advisory firm could describe itself as "Greenfield – providing independent advice on ethical products" but cannot call itself "Greenfield Independent Financial Advisers."

Furthermore, many advisers use platforms to manage their clients' assets, but not all investments are necessarily available via each platform. In such cases, an IFA must still consider any type of investment but that doesn't mean that they can't continue to use a platform for the majority of their clients, if suitable. It does mean, however, that an IFA who receives a client for whom a particular investment may be deemed to be appropriate but this investment is unavailable on their usual platform, then they must review this investment or refuse to take on the client.

2b) Restricted

An adviser who considers all investment products from all providers with the exception of one type of product (for example they may exclude religious investments such as Christian or Islamic funds) are being labelled 'restricted' since they're not offering 'whole-of-market' advice. At the other end of the spectrum, an adviser who considers only Christian and Islamic funds will also be a known as a restricted adviser. Similarly, if an adviser only considers products from a select group of providers, such as funds from Fidelity, M&G and Standard Life, for example, then they must also be known as offering restricted advice.

So is 'restricted' advice a negative thing? It's clear to see that there may be situations in which restricted financial advice might better suit your needs. An individual determined to invest within a strict set of morals may prefer to go to an expert in that field. Why turn to someone whose knowledge is spread across the entire market when you only want advice on one area?

There are varying levels of restricted advice. Restricted could mean that you never look at Structured Products as an option but are happy to look at everything else; but it could also mean that you only look at products from a small range of fund management houses.

Restricted is not 'bad' but investors need to know how the adviser is restricted and decide from there if they are happy with those restrictions.

Despite some confusion—and debate—over the nuances of 'independent' versus 'restricted' and what this means for end investors, the advice industry has largely welcomed a move to more transparent advice and a clearer fee structure.

Fees versus commission?

As a financial planner, I have operated with both – I started my professional life as a commission-only adviser with Allied Dunbar, then moved to a position where I was remunerated with a mix of fees and commission; and eventually twigged that the best way to operate is providing advice and service in return for an agreed fee and operating a transparent remuneration model.

The new rules that were brought in on 1st January 2013 mean that a product provider can no longer pay advisers "commission" where there is an investment element. In other words, putting it crudely, the likes of Prudential and Standard Life cannot pay commission to your financial adviser for selling you one of their investments or pension plans.

Advisers are now required to agree a fee for any implementation work and on-going review and service and provide you with the option of either paying that fee directly to the adviser or authorising the product provider to pay the agreed fee from the amount invested with them – this is called 'customer agreed remuneration' or 'adviser charging.'

Whichever method you choose, there is now transparency with regard to the way in which your adviser is remunerated. I believe this to be a good thing.

Professional financial planners and finance advisers have been operating as 'fee charging' advisers for many years.

You have to accept that your financial planner or financial adviser needs to be remunerated for their wisdom, the value they add and the work that they undertake on your behalf.

I am firmly of the view that it has always been far better to agree a fee with your adviser or planner and ensure that all investments are implemented on a £nil commission basis. The main advantages are:

o   It has the effect of reducing charges down to the lowest possible level on your investments and pensions, which in turn has a positive effect upon the long-term investment performance.

o   It enables you to make a value judgement because you will know what advice and service is being provided and you will know what you are paying for that advice and service. You will know whether you are receiving value for money; and if you don't feel that you are, then you are able to discuss the issue with your adviser or planner. It may be that he or she is providing value that you are not aware of or it may be that the fees are too high, in which case you are able to renegotiate the level of remuneration or move to another adviser.

o   It removes any hint of bias or vested interest. If you have agreed a fee for the advice, implementation and on-going service, the remuneration is set. So, the adviser or planner will have no vested interest in recommending any particular investment or pension plan. Please bear in mind that your financial planner needs to make a profit, because without that profit there is no incentive for them to be in business and they need cash resource to continue to invest in new technologies and new capabilities that ultimately benefit you, the client!

Chapter 5

Stage 5: The Impact Report™

It is important for your financial planner or financial adviser to provide a written summary of the advice provided and any actions taken, together with reasons why those actions have been taken. This has been generically referred to as a 'reasons why letter' and a 'suitability letter' in the past.

At Matrix Capital, we provide our clients with The Impact Report™, which provides a written summary of the advice and recommendations provided, the actions taken and the impact upon your situation. For example, if we are focussing on retirement planning the report will show the impact of the actions taken (e.g. a pension contribution) on your projected retirement income.

There are a number of important reasons and benefits to you having a written summary at this stage in the advice process:

1) The FCA as a bare minimum require your adviser to provide you with a written statement explaining why certain actions have been taken. Incidentally, you are not required to sign the document but many advisers will ask you to sign a copy of the document to confirm that you have received it.

2) The advice process, particularly if you have a complex set of circumstances, may have taken several weeks to complete. The Impact Report™ provides an opportunity for you to remain fully engaged in the process and to understand the reasons why certain recommendations have been made. In other words, you may start to lose sight of the original objectives – so it can be very useful to see it in black and white.

3) It can be very easy to assume that you are 'all sorted' when you are not. The actions that you have taken may well have closed the gap between where you would otherwise end up and where you would

like to be. However, it is probable that there is still work to do, even after implementing the initial advice. A well drafted Impact Report™ will provide you with an update as to what needs to be addressed at future review meetings in order for you to achieve your lifetime objective.

4) In the claims conscious world that we live in, you will find that your adviser's Professional Indemnity Insurers (PII) will make it a requirement of their policy that some form of written suitability statement is provided for any implementation work carried out.

5) It's very much seen as best practice to confirm advice and recommendation in some form of written report that is hopefully in plain English. It acts as a permanent record, which may be useful for both you and your adviser in future.

6) Other professional advisers, such as your accountant and solicitor may find the report useful in determining how their advice dovetails with the advice that your financial planner or financial adviser has provided. In any event, your solicitor and accountant will need to ensure that their advice is provided based upon a full understanding of your current circumstances and the background to actions that have already been taken.

So, expect your financial planner or financial adviser to provide you with a written summary at time that he or she effects a transaction for you. This is to be welcomed, because it benefits you.

Chapter 6

Stage 6: The Planning Review Programme™

One of the big disadvantages of the old system of commissions being paid to your financial planner or adviser for effecting a transaction for the client (e.g. setting up an investment or a pension) is that it placed the emphasis on the initial advice instead of the ongoing service.

Commissions paid by providers for setting up investments and pensions didn't serve the clients well; and didn't meet the needs of the adviser very well either. They created cross-subsidy because the revenue generated on initial advice and implementation was being used to pay for ongoing advice and service. Also, large transactions were being used to subsidise smaller transactions for other clients. In my opinion, it was a good thing when commissions were banished to the bin.

It is worth stating that many firms of financial planners and financial advisers have been operating a 'fee only' advisory service for many years and rebating commissions or offsetting them against client fees; and thus creating transparency, accountability and fairness. In other words, the outcomes of RDR have really only embraced existing good practice.

The Planning Review Programme™ is the on-going service and review that is made available to clients

This is where most of the value is created for you, the client.

The first 5 stages are really about understanding your aspirations, establishing a plan of action and making sure that you have optimised your financial position. I often say to clients that Stages 1-5 are about making sure that you have your financial affairs in the right boxes and that Stage 6 is all about what goes on inside the box.

To illustrate my point, we took on a client some years ago. He is typical of many new clients, in that he had an existing pension plan that had been set up some years before he approached us. When we carried out our initial analysis of his pension, we calculated that the growth on the fund had averaged 3% per annum since inception; and that he would have achieved twice that return had he received an annual review of the asset allocation and fund selection within his pension plan. It wasn't so much that his money was in the wrong box (although that was also true in his particular case) it was that no attention had been paid to what was happening inside the box.

This reinforced the view that it is the ongoing, year in year out, review and servicing that generates the most value for clients.

What does good service look like?

Most professional firms will offer a well-defined service proposition to their clients, which will include an annual review meeting, rebalancing of investments, newsletter and so forth. Also, most firms will have more than one level of service to cater to the different needs of their clients.

As an example, a good service proposition will include:

- Annual financial review meeting
- Annual investment review
- Regular newsletter
- Budget Report and tax tables
- Back-office administration
- Access to a financial planner

The two main components to The Planning Review Programme™ are the Annual Financial Review Meeting and the Annual Investment Review; and I will explain these in more detail now.

Annual Financial Review Meeting

This is your opportunity to take time out from your busy life and reflect on where you are now and what you would like to achieve. My suggestion is that you undertake this process in your financial planner's office rather than in your office or home. It's easier to control distractions when you are away from your own environment.

Preparation

There are things that I would suggest that you do and there are things that your financial planner will be doing in the background in preparation for your meeting.

It makes the meeting far more productive and meaningful if both parties have fully prepared for the meeting. In particular, it is really helpful if as much of the hard data can be updated in advance so that the discussion focussing on you and your aspirations instead of taking up time updating information such as current balances on accounts, earnings etc.

Your financial planner will be obtaining up-to-date valuations on your arrangements and creating a list of issues to discuss with you based upon changes that have occurred in the market-place, the economy, legislation and to your circumstances.

As an example, we would ask clients to complete a new Our First Conversation™ and Risk Questionnaire to make sure that we are in touch with your current aspirations, concerns and opportunities; and to elicit any changes to your risk profile.

The important thing for a financial planner is to make sure that he or she is fully up to date so as to ensure that you receive the very best in terms of advice and service at your review meeting.

Make sure that you have played your part in preparing for the meeting. You have paid for this meeting and you want to make sure that you obtain as much value as possible from the discussion.

Read all of the pre-meeting material that your financial planner sends to you and give some thought to the questions that you want answering and the issues that you consider to be important.

The financial planner will want to be clear about your objectives. All of his advice and recommendations at a review meeting will be aimed at helping you reach your stated goals in the most cost effective and time efficient manner.

The cost

There are various methods of paying for ongoing review and service, which include:

- Paying a regular trail fee as a percentage of funds under advice.
- Paying a regular retainer fee
- Paying an hourly rate fee for the financial planner's time.
- Paying a fixed fee for a review meeting, including the preparation and post-meeting work.
- A combination of the above.

Please bear in mind that good advice and service is never cheap but is always good value for money.

Be very wary of offers of a 'free financial review' because nothing is free and they are usually paid for out of a later fee or adviser charge for effecting a transaction for you. It is really important, in my view, to separate out fees for implementation work and ongoing review and service.

The meeting

Assuming that both you and your financial planner are properly prepared and you have already supplied all of the information he or she has requested, the meeting can focus on you.

The areas that you would expect to be covered are:

- Retirement planning
- Investment planning
- Estate planning and inheritance tax planning

- Income tax planning
- Capital gains tax planning
- Family and personal protection
- Business protection (if you run a business)
- Education fees planning
- Long term care planning
- Healthcare and income protection

This is a generic list of subjects because it will be tailored depending upon your circumstances and priorities.

Investment Review

This can either take place face-to-face or it can be undertaken remotely, communicating by email, post and telephone.

The process is as follows:

a) Risk profiling:

The starting point is to undertake a fresh risk profiling exercise and for the financial planner to gain an up-to-date understanding or your investment objectives.

Most firms will ask you to complete a new Risk Questionnaire. This will be divided into two parts. The first is an objective test and the second is a subjective test.

The object test considers your capacity for loss, the time horizon for your investments (i.e. when do you need access to your investment and how long do you need the income to last?) and your specific objectives for capital growth and levels of income.

The subjective test is aimed at eliciting your 'attitude to risk', which is principally establishing how you would feel if your investments fluctuated in value. You want your investments to pass the "2am test" that I referred to earlier in the book.

This is not an exact science and should only be used as a guide. However, it is an important starting point for the analysis of your existing investments and pensions; and forms the basis of the discussion that you will have with your financial planner or financial adviser.

It's important to consider the context of your risk profile. For instance, you may be quite speculative with your investment portfolio but cautious when it comes to planning for retirement. So, to ensure that your financial planner is fully informed, it's a good idea to undertake a risk profiling exercise in each area of financial planning – investments and pensions in particular.

    b)   Asset allocation:

The result of the risk profiling, and having clarity on your investment objectives, then informs the next stage, which is asset allocation.

I mentioned earlier that there are four main asset classes that make up the majority of the funds and collective investments that your financial planner would recommend.

So, asset allocation is simply making sure that you have the right mix in the right proportions. Each asset class behaves in a particular way.

Most firms will either use software for this very sophisticated process or they will outsource investment review and rebalancing to a third party investment specialist if they do not have the expertise in-house.

    c)   Fund selection:

Once the optimum asset allocation has been decided upon, the next task is to review the fund choice and rebalance the portfolio.

This involves 'drilling down' into each sector and selecting a range of funds that, when taken collectively, produces a portfolio that matches the overall volatility (i.e. Standard Deviation) suggested by the risk profiling process and targets the desired long term investment return required by you, the client. In simple terms, the aim is to balance risk and return.

What is rebalancing?

The investments in a portfolio will perform according to the market. As time goes on, a portfolio's current asset allocation will drift away from an investor's original target asset allocation (i.e. their preferred level of risk exposure). If left unadjusted, the portfolio will either become too risky, or too conservative. If it becomes too risky, that will tend to increase long-term returns, which is desirable. But when the excessive risks show up in the short term, the investor might have a tendency to do the worst possible thing at the worst possible time (i.e. sell at the bottom), thus dramatically diminishing their wealth. If the portfolio is allowed to drift to a too conservative status, then excessive short-term risk is less likely, which is desirable. However, long-term returns would also tend to be lower than desired. It is best to maintain a portfolio's risk profile reasonably close to an investor's level of risk tolerance.

The goal of rebalancing is to move the current asset allocation back in line to the originally planned asset allocation (i.e. their preferred level of risk exposure). This rebalancing strategy is specifically known as a Constant-Mix Strategy and is one of the four main dynamic strategies for asset allocation. The other three strategies are 1) Buy-and-Hold, 2) Constant-Proportion and 3) Option-Based Portfolio Insurance.

Tax considerations

There is an old adage, "don't allow the tax tail to wag the investment dog". In other words, tax should be considered but it should not drive the decisions on investments.

There are simple things that your financial planner will consider for you. For example, fully utilising your ISA allowance and your CGT allowances. CGT planning is often overlooked but can have a significant impact upon the future tax liability should you wish to encash investments. The goal is to fully utilise your CGT allowance (£11,000 2014/15) each year so that your portfolio is not 'pregnant' with gain in the future. Your CGT allowance is a 'use it or lose it' situation.

These a just examples of what goes on as part of the investment review process. Simple stuff often overlooked, but if managed on an annual basis provides significant long term value for you.

Summary

The total service proposition will undoubtedly include a review meeting along with a number of other core components.

Make sure that the service that you are receiving represents value for money and is relevant to your circumstances.

One of the issues that we have had in our practice is clients not fully appreciating the amount of work that goes on behind the scenes in order to deliver service. So much of what you financial planner does is hidden from view. We have had to become better at articulating value to our clients, so they are able to make that value judgment.

Some people want to know exactly what goes on back-stage whilst others simply want to focus on the results.

Chapter 7

Family Financial Planning

I remember years ago being at a conference and the audience asked the speaker, who was an extremely wealthy American entrepreneur, what advice he would give to someone who suddenly became a millionaire overnight as a result of receiving a legacy or winning the lottery.

His answer was, "My wish for them is that *they* become a millionaire overnight."

Of course, what he meant was that the recipient of the wealth needed to very quickly develop the mentality and the wherewithal to contend with the difficulties associated with suddenly acquiring significant wealth.

I have witnessed situations where children have inherited significant amounts of money and assets from very wealthy parents; only to see that wealth fritter away. The parents may have sacrificed many things to create that wealth; it may have taken enterprise and hard work and risk taking. Instead of that accumulated wealth being put to great use to lever advantage to improve the lives of people, it's gone.

I've met many clients in my professional life who have engaged us to provide advice and ongoing service to them as individuals or as a couple. However, particularly where they have wealthy parents and/or children themselves, we encourage them to involve both the parents and the children; and take a 'family' approach to financial planning - it's so much more effective.

I realise that there are often reasons as to why that cannot sometimes be arranged, but where it can, it does provide significant advantages.

There have been occasions during my career where it has been necessary to deal with the whole family, for example where a parent is in poor health and there needs to be agreement amongst the family members with regard to the future care of the parent and the preservation of wealth.

I realise there are potential barriers to this:

- There may be disharmony within the family.
- Privacy or secrecy may be important.
- The other family members may have their own advisers, who do not wish to collaborate.
- Lack of trust.
- Inflexible attitudes.

However, if you are able to get the family together to discuss your family's finances there are often benefits. For example, the establishment of a trust to hold assets or investments may be a suitable way of controlling who benefits from the estate, whilst meeting the needs of the settlor (i.e. the person(s) transferring assets into the trust) during their lifetime.

Trusts

Trusts can play a big part in financial planning for a family.

Let's just take a moment to understand what a trust is and what the potential uses are. I'll also articulate some the pros and cons of trusts and how you might benefits from their use.

What is a trust?

A trust is a legal concept involving the holding of property for the benefit of others. There are three main parties involved in a trust, which are:

The 'Settlor' who is the person (or persons) who creates the trust and originally owns the property, which is transferred into the trust.

The 'Trustees' are the individuals (or company) who legally own the property held within the trust, which is administered for the benefit of the beneficiaries. The settlor is sometimes the trustee.

The 'Beneficiaries' are those who can receive benefits from the trust. The beneficiaries can be named at outset or may simply be among a class of potential beneficiaries.

There is sometimes a 4th element to the relationship - a 'Protector', which is more applicable to non-UK resident (i.e. offshore) trusts than UK trusts. The protector does not hold the property like a trustee, instead his/her role is more reactive and to make sure that the trustees adhere to the settlor's wishes. For example, the protector would typically have the power to replace trustees if he or she felt that the trustees were not considering the settlor's wishes.

A trust may be established by 'deed' or may arise automatically without a deed, for example where a minor child is left a legacy in a Will or through intestacy.

To fully understand what a trust is, it may be easier to consider what a trust is not.

For example, a trust differs from a contract in that a contract is a "two-way" agreement. With a trust, there is no agreement between the settlor and the beneficiary.

A trust also differs from a company in that a company is a legal entity in its own right, whereas a trust is not a separate legal entity. Also, apart from Charitable Trusts, there is no register of trusts such as Companies House for Limited Companies and PLCs.

Since the introduction of The Perpetuities and Accumulations Act 2009, any new trust that came into force on or after 6th April 2010 has a single statutory perpetuity period of 125 years. Before that date, trusts had either a fixed period of perpetuity of 80 years from the date the trust was created or the lifetime of a specified person alive when the trust was created plus 21 years.

Why are trusts used in family financial planning?

The key reason is "control' or a more common phrase is "asset protection".

There are also potential tax planning opportunities but they are usually a secondary (but vitally important) consideration.

Trusts are usually put in place to protect assets from risks, which include:

- Bankruptcy
- Loss of family heirlooms and money through divorce and remarriage - although the Family Courts have in some cases, taken trust assets into consideration in financial settlements.
- Incapacity arising through ill-health
- Being too young or experienced to deal with property
- Assets being accessed by those with addictions who would otherwise use those funds to further their addictions.
- Certain tax outcomes

It is beyond the scope of this book to explain the tax treatment of trusts, and which type of trust is most suitable - that is definitely where you will need professional advice from a suitably qualified Trust and Estate Planner or a solicitor with those qualifications. However, to illustrate the possible use of trusts, I have outlined a real life scenario where a trust has been used to help families meet their needs:

A family has a child with special needs, but is not "disabled" as defined by legislation.

The concern here is that the child will never learn the value of money or be able to handle financial transactions. The wills of the parents include a discretionary trust from which the child can benefit. That means that on their deaths, no property needs to be transferred directly to that child, and payments can be made by the trustees, as and when they are required, or even a house purchased, without the beneficiary needing to be involved in the paperwork or the transaction.

Chapter 8

Some Financial Explanations

Risk

Let's just consider risk for a moment because it can mean different things to different people.

There are inherent risks in different asset classes, or investment types. The four main asset classes used in collective investments such as pensions and ISAs are:

> Property
> Equities (i.e. shares)
> Fixed interest (i.e. gilts and corporate bonds)
> Cash

Each of these asset classes behaves in a different way. So, one of the ways in which you can assess the risk associated with an investment is to consider the mix of underlying assets. For example, a stocks and shares ISA may have all four.

Property has the potential to grow in value over time (i.e. it can provide capital growth) and generate income (i.e. rent). You have probably purchased a home at some point in your life, so you will appreciate that it can go up in value and it can fall in value depending upon market and economic conditions. You will also know that property has the potential to generate rental income for the investor.

The risks are obvious in that the capital value can fall and the tenant may default or the property remains empty, which means that it generates no income. If you have taken out a mortgage to acquire property, the interest rates may rise, there may also be costly repairs or damage to the property by tenants that needs dealing with.

Liquidity with property is also an important consideration because property does not generally sell quickly. If you compare property to FTSE100 shares, there is a very efficient market that allows shares to be disposed of very quickly and turned in to cash – a few minutes in some cases. Whereas property has to be marketed and advertised, the buyer may want it professionally surveyed and there are legal procedures to go through, which invariably take weeks if not months.

Equities (or shares) are very similar in nature in that the value of the business that you own shares in may fall or even disappear; and the Company may not issue dividends. Conversely there is the possibility that shares in a Company may rise significantly over time and pay high dividends consistently year in year out.

Fixed Interest, which includes gilts and corporate bonds, can also fall in value and income yields can fall as well as rise. Gilts are simply loans to a government – UK Gilts are probably the safest because the UK Government has never defaulted on its obligations, unlike Greece which would default if it were not for the financial bailouts granted by the European Central Bank.

Corporate Bonds are very similar to gilts expect that the borrower is a corporate body instead of a government – Marks and Spencer for example will have raised funds for their business on the bond markets and taken out loans at agreed rates of interest and on agreed repayment terms. Corporate Bonds are generally deemed to be riskier than Government backed gilts because businesses are more likely to default than governments – consequently; the yields are normally higher to compensate the lender for taking that additional risk.

Cash carries a different type of risk – inflationary risk.

History has demonstrated that, over the long term, cash has never been able to keep pace with inflation. Consequently, if you hold cash for any length of time, its value will be eroded by inflation. That's simply because the buying power of your cash will reduce if inflation exceeds interest rates.

Cash does have its advantages though. Liquidity and ease of access are probably top of the list. Apart from the effects of inflation, the capital is relatively safe as long as its deposited with a bank or building society – Please be aware of the Financial Services Compensation Scheme (FSCS) limits because banks have gone bust and your cash is only protected up to certain limits. There is one exception to this, the NS&I Direct Saver Account which enjoys 100% protection.

Make sure that you have enough cash set aside to deal with short-term expenditure and emergencies. Entrepreneurs and business owners take risks, even though most of them would tell you they are very cautious! That means that they sometimes make decisions that put them in situations where they need cash very quickly – that can be because they need to dig themselves out of a hole or an opportunity has arisen and they need cash to take advantage. So if your life is such that these situations can arise, then I suggest you keep more than enough cash at your disposal and don't lock up your investments in a way that makes it difficult to get access to your funds.

What approach do professional financial planners take with their clients?

There are certain principles that they adopt as part of the advice process and in providing on-going review. There are also key factors in making sure that your investments are established and managed effectively.

These include:

- Risk Profile and attitude to risk
- Asset allocation
- Diversification
- Liquidity
- Tax
- Circumstances
- Needs and aspirations

Risk Profile

In my opinion 'risk profile' differs from 'attitude to risk' – attitude to risk forms part of someone's risk profile.

As referred to above, your 'risk profile' is broken down into two types of test. The first is objective and the second is subjective. There are plenty of 'risk profiling' tools available on the Internet and to professional advisers.

The objective components include things like capacity for loss and time horizon. Common sense prevails here; and it can be calculated with a degree of accuracy.

An elderly widow, who is relying upon her savings to provide all of her retirement income would probably have a very low capacity for loss because if the value of her savings suddenly dropped, she is likely to suffer financial hardship in consequence. On the other hand, a highly paid professional person, many years from retirement, is more likely to have a higher capacity for loss because he or she will have time and resources to recover financially.

Time horizon is about when do you need to access the money, how you need the funds (e.g. lump sum or income) and how long does it need to last. With reasoned and reasonable assumptions, this can be worked out fairly accurately.

The subjective components of your risk profile are essentially about your attitude to risk, how you feel about the way in which your investments behave. If you assume that you have only selected investments with financially strong institutions that are professionally managed, what you should focus on is your feelings about volatility – in other words the extent to which they rise and fall in value over time.

Asset allocation

The next step is to create an asset allocation that is based upon your risk profile.

Asset allocation is just the mix of investment types – usually the four already mentioned - property, equities, fixed interest and cash.

In other words, what proportion of your investment is going to be placed into each asset class? Now you can get very technical with this process; and there are a number of software packages that will create the 'optimum' asset allocation based upon your risk profile and investment objectives (i.e. whether you want capital growth, income or a bit of both).

I believe that it is this stage in the process that is mainly responsible for the long-term investment performance of your portfolio.

Whether you employ a professional adviser to do this for you or do it yourself, you should aim to structure the mix of assets in such a way that the overall investment performance potential and the volatility are pretty closely aligned with your own personal risk profile.

This can be done more easily if you are using collective or 'pooled' investments, such as unit trusts, investment trusts and open-ended investment companies (OEICs) because there is lots of data on the past performance and volatility ratios of these types of funds. It's extremely difficult, if not impossible, to gather accurate date on individual direct investments into property or shares for instance.

A collective investment is a fund where lots of other investors have pooled their money; and a fund manager has then invested in a range of asset classes to create diversification.

The benefits of collective investments are as follows:

Professional expertise – an investment expert makes the investment choices for you, monitor those investments and judge when to buy and when to sell.

Spreading your risk – even if you have a small amount to invest, you can spread your money across a wide range of investments, asset classes and economies around the World.

Reduced dealing costs – if you want to buy a range of investments directly, you might only be able to invest a relatively small sum in each. The dealing costs could eat into your profits, whereas you benefit from bulk buying.

Less administration – the fund manager deals with buying, selling and collecting of dividend income for you. They also deal with foreign exchange and brokers, which can be tricky and time consuming.

Choice – there is a wide choice of funds

Once the asset allocation has been established, the next step is the selection of individual investments and/or funds.

There is a lot of information freely available on the Internet on individual funds; the fund managers will fall over themselves to provide data and historic performance figures for their particular funds. However, you do need to find a way of assimilating all of the information and putting together a selection of investments that meet your asset allocation criteria.

I suggest you take professional advice on this issue and ignore what you read, hear and see. A financial planner will have access to fund selection software that will ensure that your fund selection is prepared properly and the investments themselves are implemented correctly and in the agreed proportions.

Diversification

This is the old adage, "don't have all your eggs in one basket." It is a basic tool for risk management at your disposal.

Collective investments help enormously with diversification because you can very quickly and easily spread your investment across different asset classes, different fund managers and different geographic regions. Whether you use collective investments or direct investment into particular investments (e.g. property purchase) you will need to create a sufficient spread with your money to try and manage the overall volatility of your portfolio.

Also, you need to be aware that when one investment class is performing well, another is not performing well. For example, interests may rise making cash a very attractive investment; and in consequence businesses (and therefore equities) may perform poorly because the cost of borrowing has increased. This is another compelling reason for spreading your investments across different asset classes.

Chapter 9

Tax Planning

Whilst taxation is a factor when deciding upon investments, and how those investments are held, it should not be the only or main reason for investing.

That said, there are 'tax reducing' and 'tax efficient' investments that may be worth considering. **Tax reducing** investments include pension contributions, Enterprise Investment Schemes (EIS) Seed Enterprise Investment Schemes (SEIS) and Venture Capital Trusts (VCT).

Tax efficient investments include such things as Individual Savings Accounts (ISAs) Junior ISAs, friendly society plans and maximum investment plans.

Some of the opportunities, such as EIS and VCT, carry significant risk and are sometimes complicated. However, there is some simple stuff that works.

One of the most popular tax reducing investments is a **pension contribution**:

These are considered tax reducing because, under current legislation, tax relief is available on contributions made into a 'registered' pension fund in the UK; and tax relief is available to almost everyone, even non-tax payers.

Basic rate tax relief is granted at source for non-taxpayers. So, even if you do not currently pay tax because your total taxable income is within the personal allowance, you still enjoy tax relief on the amount you invest in your pension fund.

'At source' means that you receive the basic rate tax relief upfront and this tax relief is then reclaimed by your pension provider from HMRC and is paid directly into your pension fund and added to the net amount paid by you personally.

There are limits to the amount that you are able to pay in each year and claim tax relief on (the greater of £3,600 or 100% of your earned income and subject to the annual allowance of £40,000 (2014/14)); and there is a limit on the total amount that you are able to accumulate in all of your pension funds without incurring a tax charge – the limit is called the 'Lifetime Allowance' which is currently £1.25m (2014/15).

Here's an example of how your tax relief works if you are a non taxpayer or a basic rate tax payer, paying into your own fund from your own bank account:

Your net contribution (i.e. the cash amount that you invest)	£2,880
Tax relief credited to your fund from HMRC	£720
Total gross amount invested in your pension fund	**£3,600**

If you are a 'higher' rate or an 'additional' rate taxpayer, you are entitled to tax relief at those rates on some or all of your contributions; and using the figures from above, it works like this for a higher rate tax payer (40% in 2014/15) who has at least £3,600 of income on which he pays higher rate tax:

Total gross pension contribution	£3,600
Tax relief at 40%	£1,440
Less: tax relief granted at source	(£720)
Remaining higher rate tax relief due	£720

The higher rate tax relief is either given to you by way of a tax refund from HMRC or by way of an adjustment to your PAYE code.

The principle is the same for 'additional' rate taxpayers, paying tax at the rate of 45% (2014/15).

Using your **Annual Capital Gains Tax (CGT) Exemption** is very simple and often overlooked:

Make sure that you crystallise a 'gain' on your investments each year to fully utilise your annual exemption (£11,000 2014/15) by creating a disposal and then reinvesting, taking care not to fall into the trap of 'bed and breakfasting' your investments. The effect of successfully crystallising a gain is that the 'acquisition price' on the investments is lifted each year to the current value.

When you eventually dispose of your portfolio, it will not be pregnant with gain and lead to a significantly greater CGT liability than would otherwise be the case had you carried out this exercise for each of the previous years. Your CGT Exemption cannot be carried forwards, so it is a case of use it or lose it.

Moving income generating assets to a spouse that is paying income tax at a lower rate:

A simple example is a higher rate taxpayer with a basic rate taxpayer spouse. Transferring deposit accounts and asset-backed investments, such as unit trusts and OEICs to the spouse paying basic rate income tax will reduce the overall income tax liability for the household.

There is no CGT on transfer of assets between spouses, however the original acquisition price remains unaltered. In other words, the acquisition price is not rebased to current value as part of the exercise. But if the basic rate taxpaying spouse subsequently disposes of the asset and the total gain, when added to income, is totally within the basic rate band, the CGT rate of tax will be 18% instead of 28% (2014/15) on the gain.

The transfer of assets between spouses needs careful planning and professional advice because there are a number of factors that have to be taken into account before making the decision.

If you run your own business, **restructuring your remuneration** may be a very simple way of reducing the overall income tax and National Insurance liabilities for the household:

A shareholding director of a Limited Company (or indeed a PLC) is usually able to extract profits from his or her business in one of three ways – PAYE salary or bonus, dividends and pension contributions.

You may be in the position of being both employer and employee and able to structure the way in which you are remunerated. Getting the balance between PAYE, dividends and pension contributions is very important; and needs to be considered from both your point of view and that of your co-directors/shareholders and the company itself.

A fully qualified financial planner or accountant would have software that will enable you to determine the optimum mix of salary, dividends and pension contribution. However, I have summarised the key differences and the possible planning opportunities below:

PAYE attracts Class 1 National Insurance Contributions for both the Company and you as an employee. The rate for the Company (2014/15) is 13.8% on all 'earnings' above £153 per week (uncapped).

For you as an employee, the rate is 12% on 'earnings' above £153 per week and then 2% on earnings above £805 per week, again uncapped.

From the Company's point of view, your 'earnings' and NICs paid by them on those earnings, are tax deductible in that they will appear on the Company's profit and loss statement as an item of deductible business expenditure (assuming of course that your salary and bonuses were incurred, "wholly and exclusively in the pursuit of trade").

Dividends are distributions made by the company to its shareholders, and are a share of net profits of the Company. So, they can only be paid if the Company has distributable profits either from the current year or retained on the balance sheet from previous years' profits.

There is no NIC for either the employer or the employee on dividend payments, but they must be paid in the same proportion as the shareholding. However, dividends may be waived under certain circumstances. They are not a tax-deductible expense for the business because the Company is merely distributing profits to shareholders.

The key reason for shareholding directors being paid dividends instead of PAYE salary or bonuses is the saving in NIC.

Pension contributions made by the Company into a pension arrangement for the shareholding director (or indeed any employee) are a very tax efficient method of extracting profits from the Company for the benefit of the individual.

Pension contributions paid by the Company do not trigger an NIC charge for either the Company itself or the individual. Also, within the allowable limits, it will not trigger a tax charge for the individual – in other words, a pension contribution would not create an income tax charge for the individual.

From the Company's point of view, as long as the pension contribution passes the "wholly and exclusively..." test, it will appear as a deductible business expense and full corporation tax relief will apply to the contribution.

In other words, pension contributions can be very tax efficient for both the shareholding director and the Company; but you do have to bear in mind that there are some restrictions and rules surrounding pensions that will require professional advice from a Chartered Financial Planner.

There is a balance to be struck between tax-efficiency and achieving the right level of net income and providing for retirement.

Summary

Having read the book, you should now have the knowledge, tools and the motivation to review your own financial position more objectively.

You should have decided upon your 3 most important lifetime aspirations, identified your biggest concerns, grasped the most inspiring opportunities and unearthed your innate strengths and know how to use them.

You should also understand how a Chartered Financial Planner can get incredible results, where to find one and what questions to ask before engaging a professional wealth manager.

The Financial Empowerment Programme provides you with a logical six step process that you can use to understand where you are, what you've got and what needs to be done to achieve your goals.

The '5 Dials' are the vital things to monitor on your journey of creating, protecting and passing on your wealth.

I hope the payoff for you is that a few myths have been dispelled, beliefs challenged and wealth management simplified down to a logical process. The outcome should be that you have a robust financial plan that enables you to enjoy the two most important freedoms:

1) Freedom to not do what you do not want to do and;

2) Freedom to do what you want to do

Glossary

Accrual Rate - The rate at which your pension benefits build up as pensionable service is completed in a Final Salary Pensions Scheme, which is also known as a Defined Benefit Scheme. The accrual rate may, for example, be 1/60th of your pensionable earnings for each year of service. So, 30 years' service would provide a pension of 30/60th (i.e.1/2) of your pensionable earnings at retirement.

Actuary - Someone professionally qualified to consider financial issues, particularly ones involving probabilities such as life expectancy.

AER - (Annual Equivalent Rate) The interest paid from current, deposit or savings accounts.

Annual volatility - A measure used to assess the risk of a portfolio.

Annuity - This is the contract you purchase from an insurance company using a lump sum of money (e.g. the proceeds of your pension fund) to guarantee you an annual income for a fixed period of time (e.g. for ten years) or for life.

APR - (Annual Percentage Rate) the percentage rate, taking account of charges over a year, you are charged on the outstanding balance when you borrow money or make a purchase on credit.

Assets - Anything of value can be referred to as an asset, such as your home, jewellery or antiques.

AVCs - (Annual Voluntary Contributions) Extra payments you can make in addition to your main occupational pension scheme contributions to boost your retirement benefits. AVCs can be paid either to your employer's scheme or to a separate arrangement. See also FSAVCs

Base rate - The interest rate set by the Bank of England on which other banks base their rates.

Basic Rate Tax - The income tax paid on taxable income above a certain figure, currently 20%.

Basic State Pension - the single person's flat rate State pension paid when you reach state pension age assuming you have paid sufficient National Insurance contributions during your working life.

Bid-offer spread - The difference between the prices at which you buy units and sell them back.

Bid price - The price at which you sell units in a unit trust back to the investment manager.

Bonus - An extra payment that with-profits policyholders may have added to their contract depending on the profits the company makes in any one year, or over a period of years.

Capital - A lump sum of money.

Capital Gains Tax - The tax payable on profit made on the sale of assets or property other than your principal place of residence.

Capital growth - An increase in the value of shares or other assets in a fund.

Capital and Interest Mortgage - A mortgage product where the payment you make each month covers the capital and interest on your loan.

Commission - The means by which financial advisers or salespeople are paid by an insurance company for placing business with them.

Contracting in/out - The process by which you can elect to stay in or opt out of the State Second Pension.

Corporate bond - A form of investment offered by a corporation with the purpose of raising capital, in which the lump sum is repaid with interest at maturity. In other words, loans to companies, which can be bought and sold on the stock market.

Corporation tax – Tax on profits paid by Limited Companies (Ltd) and Public Limited Companies (Plc)

Critical illness insurance - Pays a lump sum upon diagnosis of a defined illnesses or permanent disability (e.g. certain forms of cancer, heart attack, and stroke). The policy usually pays out after surviving 28 days after diagnosis

Death after Retirement Benefits - The pension and lump sum paid to the deceased member's spouse and/or other dependants where death occurs after retirement or after the member's normal retirement date if s/he is retiring late.

Death in Service Benefits - The pension and lump sum paid to the deceased member's spouse and/or other dependants where death occurs while still working for his/her employer, before his/her normal retirement date.

Debit card – Payments made on debit cards are deducted directly from your bank.

Deed of Covenant - An agreement in a deed to transfer income from one person to another.

Defined Benefit Scheme - Also known as a Final Salary Scheme. An occupational pension scheme where your pension is calculated as a proportion of your salary based upon the Accrual Rate.

Defined Contribution Scheme - Also known as a Money Purchase Scheme. A scheme where the amount of a member's retirement benefits depends on the contributions paid into the scheme in respect of the member and investment performance.

Distribution - Payments made to investors of income generated by an investment fund.

Dividend - The distribution to shareholders of a company's profits in proportion to the number of shares held.

Endowment Policy – A combined life assurance and savings policy, which pays an amount of money at the end of an agreed term or a specified amount on death of the life assured.

Equities – Shares in a company.

EURO - The currency adopted by some European countries in place of their national currencies.

FCA - The Financial Conduct Authority, the main regulator of the financial services industry. Previously, the Financial Services Authority (FSA).

Final Salary Scheme – Also known as Defined Benefit Scheme.

Fiscal Policy – Taxation policies aimed at improving the economic circumstances.

Fixed Rate Mortgage - A mortgage product where your monthly payments do not change over a agreed period.

Flexible Mortgage - A mortgage product where you can vary the amount you pay each month, reduce the term by making extra or increased payments and take breaks from your monthly payments.

FTSE 100 - The name for the Financial Times Stock Exchange 100, the main UK share index which represents the prices of the top 100 shares in public limited companies.

FSAVCs - Free Standing Additional Voluntary Contributions, which are extra payments you can make into an individual plan, which runs alongside your company pension scheme, to top up your pension fund. The plan is independent of your employer's main pension scheme.

Fund - General term for an investment vehicle which pools the money of investors.

Fund Manager - A professional who makes the day-to-day decisions on what to buy and sell on behalf of a fund's investors, in line with the objectives of the fund.

Fundamentals - The underlying economic factors such as industry output, wages, cost of materials and fluctuations in currency, which affect a market, country or sector.

FURBS - Funded Unapproved Retirement Benefits Schemes. This is an occupational pension scheme that does not offer attractive tax benefits but equally has fewer restrictions

Futures - A contract to buy or sell a fixed amount of currencies, shares or commodities at a fixed rate in the future at a fixed price.

Gilt - Gilt Edged Security. A fixed-interest bond or security issued by the British Government. In simple terms, it is a loan to the Government.

GPP - Group Personal Pension. An arrangement made for employees of a particular employer to participate in a personal pension scheme on a group basis.

Hedging - A strategy designed to manage investment risk.

IFA - Independent Financial Adviser. An IFAs is a financial adviser who are able to select from all the products available in the marketplace.

Income Drawdown - Facility by which you can draw an income from your pension fund while keeping the fund fully invested.

Income Tax - Tax payable on your income.

Index - The means of measuring movement of statistics over a period of time used as a benchmark by unit trust managers.

Index-linked - Payments protected against the effects of inflation by increasing in line with the changes in the index of retail prices.

Inflation - The percentage by which prices have risen or fallen over a rolling 12 month period.

Inheritance Tax - Tax payable on the value of your assets passed to others either upon death or during your lifetime.

Initial Charge - A charge levied by your investment manager to cover administration and adviser charges when you invest in a fund.

Interest-only Mortgage - A mortgage product where you make a monthly payment that only covers the interest and does not reduce the amount borrowed.

Investment Trust - A company, quoted on the Stock Exchange, which invests in other companies' shares.

ISA - Individual Savings Account. Tax-efficient savings plans, which can hold cash or investments, or a combination of the two, which were introduced in 1999 and replaced TESSAs and PEPs.

Joint life - Joint life plans cover two (or more) people, usually a husband and wife. Benefits can be paid following the first death, or following the death of both

Keyman insurance - This provides cover, against the loss of profits a company is likely to suffer following the death of a key employee.

Liability - A debt, or amount of money, owed to others.

Listed company - A company whose shares are quoted on a recognised stock market.

Management Accounts - Accounts which are prepared for use when managing the business.

Market Capitalisation - The value of a company measured by the total stock market price of its shares, calculated by multiplying the number of shares by the current market price of a share.

Micropal Star Ratings - Micropal is an independent Mutual Fund analyst, which monitors all the UK's unit trust and OEICs and awards stars on a scale of 0-5.

Monetary Policy - Influencing an economy through control of the money supply.

Money Purchase Scheme - Also known as Defined Contribution Scheme.

Mutual company - A company which has no shareholders but is owned instead by its with-profits policyholders.

Mutual Fund - An open-ended fund operated by an investment company which raises money from shareholders and invests in a group of assets in accordance with a stated set of objectives. Shares are issued and redeemed on demand

NASDAQ - Index of the leading technology stocks in the USA.

National Insurance - Payments made out of earnings by employees, employers and the self-employed to the Government that entitle you to a state pension and other benefits.

National Insurance Rebate - The amount by which a persons National Insurance Contributions can be redirected into an Appropriate Personal Pension if contracted out of the State Second Pension (S2P).

Negative Equity - This is when the market value of your house is less than the amount outstanding on your mortgage.

Net Yield - The return on an investment after tax has been deducted.

Occupational Pension Scheme - A legal contract set up by an employer to provide pensions and/or other benefits for one or more employees on retirement, death or leaving pensionable service.

OEIC - Open Ended Investment Company. Managed funds, which hold a portfolio of investments that you can buy into. They issue shares instead of units and normally quote a single price.

Offer Price - The price at which you buy units from a unit trust manager.

Offshore Funds - Funds based outside the UK.

OMO - Open Market Option. Your right at retirement to shop around and buy an annuity from a provider other than the one who has administered your pension fund.

Option - In investment terms, a contract giving the right to buy or sell commodities, currencies or shares at a fixed date in the future at a fixed price.

PAYE - Pay As You Earn. Where income tax and National Insurance contributions are collected from your salary, before it is paid to you, by your employer and passed to HM Revenue & Customs.

Pension Forecast - A service provided by the Department of Work and Pensions which tells you what your state pension is worth.

Pensions Ombudsman -An independent arbitrator for pension disputes with statutory power to enforce his or her decisions.

Personal Pension Scheme - A pension scheme for those who wish to make their own pension provision.

Phased Retirement - The facility to use small amounts of your pension fund to buy annuities as and when you need income, rather than buying one annuity at retirement with your whole pension fund.

PHI - Permanent Health Insurance. Insurance that pays a level of income in the event that the policyholder is unable to work as a result of long-term sickness or disability.

PLC - Public Limited Company. Any company with a share capital of at least a statutory minimum.

PMI - Private Medical Insurance. Insurance which will pay for the cost of medical treatment.

Portfolio - A collection of investments owned by an investor.

Price/Earnings Ratio - Calculated by dividing the market price of a company's ordinary shares by its earning-per-share figure as an indicator of the company's performance potential.

Qualifying (life policy) - a type of insurance policy that can have preferential tax benefits.

Quartile - Most UK funds are grouped into sectors and each sector is divided into four quartiles with the best performing funds being in the top quartile.

Return - The amount by which the value of your investment increases or decreases.

Rights Issue - New shares sold by a company to raise capital.

Risk – Factors that can adversely affect the value of your investments (e.g. inflation).

RPI - Retail Price Index - The official measure of inflation calculated by weighting the costs of goods and services to approximate a typical family spending pattern.

Scrip Issue - The issue of new share certificates to existing shareholders to reflect an accumulation of profits on a company's balance sheet.

Securities - The collective name for stocks and shares.

SERPS - State Earnings Related Pension Scheme. A state pension in addition to the basic state pension based on earnings. Replaced by the State Second Pension (S2P) on 6th April 2002.

Shares - A stake in a company, which may entitle you to vote at annual meetings and benefit from the company's profits in the form of a dividend.

Small Caps - Another name for small companies.

SSAS - Small Self Administered Scheme, which is an occupational scheme where the members are trustees and are directly responsible for administering the fund and paying out the benefits. Some funds are invested in assets known as 'permitted investments'.

Stakeholder pension - Low cost pension schemes introduced by the government in 2001 to encourage people to make provision for their financial future.

Stock market - The marketplace for the sale and purchase of shares, government bonds and other securities.

Switching - Moving an investment out of one fund and into another.

Term Assurance – A life assurance contract with a fixed term and a sum assured which is paid out only if the life assured dies within the term specified.

TESSA – Tax-exempt special savings accounts replaced by ISAs in 1999. You can no longer invest in a new TESSA but you can transfer your existing TESSA into an ISA.

Tied Agent – Financial advisers who have an agreement with one particular company to recommend its products. They can range from self employed individuals to banks and building societies and can give you advice on your financial circumstances but they cannot survey the whole market for you.

Total Return – The combination of capital growth and reinvested income at the end of any given period.

Transfer Value – The amount of money which is available to be transferred to another pension or investment arrangement.

UCITS - Undertaking for Collective Investments in Transferable Securities. A Ucits fund is theoretically one that is authorised for sale in any of the EU member states.

Unit Linked Policy - An insurance policy in which the benefits depend on the performance of units in a fund invested in shares, bonds and property.

Unit Trust - An investment contract which invests in a variety of different stocks and shares and is divided into units which are issued to its members instead of shares.

Variable Rate Mortgage - A mortgage product where the amount of the monthly payment goes up or down in accordance with variations in the interest rate, normally based on the Bank of England rate.

VAT - Value Added Tax. A form of indirect taxation levied on goods and services.

Volatility - The degree by which share prices in a particular market or sector go up or down.

Whole Life Policy - A life insurance policy which pays a specified amount on the death of the life assured regardless of when death occurs.

Winding Up - The legal termination of a pension scheme.

With Profits Policy - A policy, which usually has annual bonuses added to the sum insured. On death or maturity a terminal bonus may also be applied to the fund value.

Working Capital - The amount of money required by a business to fund its day-to-day trading activities.

Work-out solutions - An informal reorganisation of the business and settlement of its affairs outside of formal insolvency proceedings.

XD - Ex-Dividend - The interval between the announcement and payment of the next dividend or, in the case of a unit trust, the next income distribution.

Yield - The annual dividend or income from an investment.

Zero Rated - Goods or services that are taxable for VAT but with a tax rate of zero.

Real Life Case Studies

Denise Horne

Managing Director of the UK arm of a very large well-known international business.

The Situation
Denise is one of our long-standing clients, having been introduced to us by one of our existing clients. At the time, Denise was the Managing Director of the UK arm of a very large well-known international business. She was, and remains, extremely busy with a demanding business schedule and was looking for a firm of financial planners that she could trust and rely upon to take care of her growing investment and pensions portfolio.

The Problem
Denise has always been well organised and financially astute; and had already accumulated significant amounts of money in her employer's pension scheme and in a variety of investment plans. However, Denise recognised that there needed to be a co-ordinated plan to ensure that her regular investments were properly aligned with her personal aspirations and would pass the "2am test" – in other words, she wanted to sleep at night. She also recognised that she was probably missing out on opportunities to manage her Income Tax liability.

How the Matrix Capital Limited team helped
We carried out a thorough examination of Denise's financial circumstances, which included her existing pension schemes, savings and investments. We also took the time to fully understand her personal aspirations and a lot of the intangible factors, such as attitude to risk, which are vitally important when advising clients. We formed the view that Denise would benefit from a written financial plan and for us to work from the ground up with her pensions and investments. There were some 'quick wins' that we were able to implement for Denise, an example of which was to utilise 'salary sacrifice' by creating significant savings in National Insurance Contributions and Income Tax,

and then using those savings to boost the performance or her pension savings. We then established Denise as a 'Private Client', which meant that she benefitted from our process of regular annual review and on-going service to make sure that her financial plan remained perfectly aligned with her ever changing circumstances and aspirations.

What the client said about Matrix Capital Limited
Over the last 5 years, investment performance has been robust and this has been through the biggest banking and stock market crisis in history. Robin and Gary have always taken care to make sure that they understand me and what I want to achieve. Having worked with them since 2005, they have demonstrated the highest levels of technical competence and ethical behaviour. Their commitment to providing professional advice and long-term service to me as a client has placed me in a position where I now have a pension fund that will provide me with a comfortable retirement. I would like to take this opportunity to say a huge "thank you" to the Matrix Capital team because they have worked extremely hard on my behalf; their 'Private Client' service is nothing short of first class.

Martyn Webster

Webster-Wilkinson Limited

The Situation

Webster-Wilkinson Limited were introduced to us by their accountant to provide them with advice on their existing pension arrangements and employee benefits. The Company had an existing Small Self-Administered Scheme (SSAS) directors' pension scheme, which owned one of the properties that the Company traded from. The Company also held a lease on a second property, which was being held over pending the conclusion of renewal negotiations. Neither the SSAS nor the staff pension scheme and employee benefits had been professionally reviewed for some time. The Company wanted to ensure that it was maximising opportunities and reducing its overheads.

The Problem

It became apparent during our early discussions that what the directors really wanted to achieve was to purchase the second unit that they were leasing from the Local Authority. However, the Local Authority had been unwilling to sell. Consequently, the directors were considering a number of alternatives including relocating the business altogether which would have required a significant financial investment and would have been very disruptive. The SSAS had not been looked after by their previous advisers and the Group Pension Scheme and Group 'Death-In-Service' Scheme were in need of an overhaul and an ongoing service strategy.

How the Matrix Capital Limited team helped

We initially established a regular review regime for the SSAS, which included the implementation of annual SSAS trustee meetings with the Scheme Administrator in attendance. We also carried out a full back-office review of their existing arrangements, which enabled us to implement changes that created significantly improved employee benefits whilst, at the same time, meeting the Company`s desire to reduce overheads. In other words we achieved greater benefits at lower cost. The second phase was to facilitate negotiations between the Local Authority and the Trustees of the SSAS relating to the sale of the freehold interest in the second property. We also provided the technical know-how and professional advice needed to arrange the funding for the property purchase by the SSAS.

What the client said about Matrix Capital Limited
Quite frankly, without Robin Melley, Gary Matthews and the team at Matrix Capital we would not have been able to achieve what we have; most significantly we have been able to purchase the second unit, which we had given up trying to persuade the local authority to sell to us. Acquiring this second property has not only secured the future of Webster-Wilkinson Limited but it has also meant that we remain a viable business and a long-standing employer in the community. What Matrix Capital has achieved for our Company is, quite simply, remarkable – they have exceeded our expectations by a very long way. They had been highly recommended by our accountants and we were impressed with their professional approach. Even so, they still managed to exceed our expectations in terms of their ability and commitment in bringing about extraordinary results for us as clients. They are highly competent, professional in every way and we really like their transparent method of charging. You know where you stand with Matrix Capital and it's very reassuring to know that you're in safe hands with very important matters that impact upon the business and the personal lives of the directors and the staff.

Adrian & Margaret Lester

The Situation
Adrian and Margaret, a successful and retired business couple, had accumulated significant wealth and were very comfortable financially. Unfortunately, Adrian had been diagnosed with Parkinson's Disease; and Margaret had become his full-time carer.

The Problem
Adrian and Margaret wanted to ensure that their affairs were properly organised and professionally managed, however, Adrian's medical condition was making it difficult to cope. There was a significant Inheritance Tax liability looming within their estate, there were no Wills in place and consequently no asset protection. Adrian and Margaret wanted to ensure that their capital was protected in such a manner so that they could enjoy the remainder of their lives without having to worry. They also wanted to ensure that their son and their grandchildren eventually benefitted from their estate, whilst at the same time ensure that their future needs for income and capital were met.

How the Matrix Capital Limited team helped
Adrian's medical condition meant speed was of the essence. Having carried out a full analysis, we developed a plan and agreed to work in collaboration with a Wills and Trusts specialist to first of all ensure that Wills were properly drafted and Lasting Powers of Attorney were established.
Their investments were arranged with the use of a Discounted Gift Trust. This provided Adrian and Margaret with a secure income and ease of administration. It also ensured that as much of their wealth as possible was held outside of their estate, significantly reducing future generations' Inheritance Tax liability and protecting the family's assets.

What the client said about Matrix Capital Limited
"Gary Matthews, Robin Melley and the whole team at Matrix Capital took away all of our concerns. They dealt with us in a very caring and sensitive manner; they took time to understand our circumstances and our aspirations. We were really impressed that they were able to

recommend and collaborate with Sue, the Wills and Trust specialist, to ensure that our investments and other assets were properly protected, Wills were established and Lasting Powers of Attorney were put in place. We feel very safe and secure now. The regular reviews give us the reassurance that everything remains on track and that adjustments are made as things change. Adrian has unfortunately worsened, and life can be tough sometimes but we feel in safe hands now and feel able to focus on our time together. We shall be forever grateful for the team at Matrix Capital taking care of the management of our savings and investments and making sure that we received robust advice".

Darren Giles

T Giles Glazing Limited

The Situation
The client's accountant initially approached us to determine if we were able to assist with a particularly knotty issue. The situation was that T Giles Glazing Limited jointly owned the trading estate from which they operated; and the co-owner was seeking to force the sale of the site to a third party in order to crystallise the value of their half share. T Giles Glazing Limited also needed to clear a business loan and required additional working capital to fund the increased levels of business they had secured.

The Problem
The co-owner of the site had started legal action to force the sale of the site; the company needed capital to repay the loan and to fund the increased levels of new orders. Their existing bank was unwilling to assist as the sector that T Giles Glazing Limited operated in was now outside of their lending policy – this was despite the Company having been a very good longterm customer. Neither T Giles Glazing Limited nor the directors had sufficient capital with which to acquire the co-owner's half share and to meet the needs of the business.

How the Matrix Capital Limited team helped
Fortunately the directors each had personal pension arrangements, some of which had been 'frozen'
for some years. Matrix Capital Limited first established a Small Self-Administered Scheme (SSAS) for T Giles Glazing Limited. The directors' individual pension funds were then transferred into the SSAS, which then established a loan with a new bank. This provided the funding to enable the pension scheme to acquire both of the half shares – one from T Giles Glazing Limited and the second from the co-owner. The end result was that the legal action was stopped. The whole trading estate is now safely locked away in the directors' pension scheme and T Giles Glazing Limited were provided with sufficient funds from the sale proceeds of the site to clear their loan and fund the working capital requirements created by the increased level of orders from customers.

A formal lease has been established between the SSAS and T Giles Glazing Limited, who sub-let the parts of the site not used by them; this provides additional profit and cash flow to support the main trading activities of T Giles
Glazing Limited.

What the client said about Matrix Capital Limited
Darren Giles, the Managing Director for T Giles Glazing Limited, said, "We were in a ridiculous situation as we had a really healthy order book and a good relationship with our bank. However, we were peering into the abyss financially and being placed under huge pressure to vacate the site so the co-owner could get his hands on some cash. Robin Melley and the rest of the team at Matrix Capital knew exactly how to navigate through the jungle that we found ourselves in and came up with a really innovative way of getting the result that we wanted. I can't really put into words how we feel about Robin and the Matrix Capital team but I'll have a go: In my opinion, they are the consummate professionals; they are technically spot on, they always did what they said they would do and went way beyond our expectations. It was refreshing to deal with a firm that we never once had to chase – they were continually thinking ahead of us and taking actions before we could blink. The whole team displayed a "can do" attitude about any problem or situation that arose along the way – and it was by no means a straight-forward matter to deal with. They took ownership throughout and hand held it through to a satisfactory conclusion. When I look back, they have really done an amazing thing for us; the whole mess has been transformed into something wonderful – the business is now on a firm financial footing and we are able to move the business forwards. We are definitely in safe hands with Matrix Capital.

This publication is for general information only and is not intended to be advice to any specific person. You are recommended to seek competent professional advice before taking or refraining from taking any action on the basis of the contents of this publication.

The Financial Conduct Authority (FCA) does not regulate tax advice, so this is outside the investment protection rules of the Financial Services and Markets Act and the Financial Services Compensation Scheme. This publication represents our understanding of law and HM Revenue & Customs practice as at 23/02/15.

Notes Space

Made in the USA
Charleston, SC
29 April 2015